Vigil & Vision. New Sonnets by John Payne

John Payne was born on 23rd August 1842 in Bloomsbury, London.

He began his career in the legal profession but thus was soon put to one side as he began his renowned translations of Boccaccio's Decameron, The Arabian Nights, and then the poets Omar Khayyam, François Villon and Diwan Hafez. Of the latter, who he ranked in the same bracket as Dante and Shakepeare, he said; he takes the "whole sweep of human experience and irradiates all things with his sun-gold and his wisdom"

Later Payne became involved with limited edition publishing, and the Villon Society, which was dedicated to the poems of François Villon who was Frances' best known poet of the middle Ages and unfortunately also a thief and a murderer.

John Payne died on 11ᵗʰ February, 1916 at the age of 73 in South Kensington, London.

Index of Contents

I.

SIGNS AND SEASONS

THE MONTHS

JANUARY

This is the bitter birth-month of the year.
The sun looms large against the leaden sky,
Rayless and red, as 'twere a giant's eye,
That through the mists of death abroad doth peer:
The fettered earth is dumb for frosty cheer,
Veiling its face to let the blast go by.
Who said, "Spring cometh"? Out upon the lie!
Spring's dead and buried: January's here.
Shut to the door; heap logs upon the fire.
If in your heart there harbour yet some heat,
Some sense of flowers and light and Summer-sweet,
In some half-fabulous dream of days foregone
Remembered, feed withal hope's funeral pyre,
So you may live to look upon the dawn.

FEBRUARY

How long, O Lord, how long the Winter's woes?
I it to purge the world of sin and stain

That in its winding-sheet it stands again
For penance, pining in the shrouded snows?
Methinks, I do remember of the rose
To have heard fable in some far domain
Of old fantastic dreams and fancies vain;
But what in sooth it was, God only knows'
Was ever aught but Winter in the land
Was ever snow time past and Springtime come,
To bless the brown earth with her flowerful hands?
Well nigh the cuckoo's call, the wild bee's hum
Have we forgot. Vet, through the chill snow-cope,
The kindly crocus blooms and bids us hope.

MARCH

March comes at last, the labouring lands to free.
Rude blusterer, with thy cloud-compelling blast,
The pining plains from cark of Winter past
That clear'st and carpetest each bush and tree
With daffodil and wood-anemone,
A voice from the illimitable Vast
Of dreams thou art, the tale that doth forecast
Of hope yet live and happiness to be.
And hark, the robin fluting on the bough,
The rough breeze tangling on his tender breast
The ruddy plumes! Yet sings he, unopprest,
The awakening year, the blessed burgeoning
In wood and weald, the Then becoming Now
And all the pleasant presage of the Spring.

APRIL

Sweet April, with thy mingling tears and smiles,
Dear maid-child of the changing months that art,
What wit so blunt, what breast with sorrow's smart
So sore but must confess thy tender wiles?
What woes but thy capricious charm beguiles?
At thy sweet sight, the winter-thoughts depart
And with glad lips men say and gleeful heart,
"Belike we yet shall greet the Golden Isles".
Pale as thy primrose, as thy violets sweet,
Thy varying stint thou fill'st of dainty days;
Yet, though thy bright prime passeth, still shall praise
And blessing follow on thy flitting feet

Nor Summer's sheen thy memory make less dear,
That bring'st the first-fruits of the flowering year.

The wild bird carolled all the April night,
Among the leafing limes, as who should say,
"Lovers, have heed; here cometh in your May,
"When you shall walk in woods and heart's delight
"Have in the fresh-flowered fields and Spring's sweet sight!"
And truly, with the breaking of the day,
Came the glad month and all the world was gay
With lilac-breath and blossoms red and white.
Oh moon of love, how shall the snowtide do
To wind the world again with winter-death,
Whilst in our hearts the thought of thee is blent
With memories more sweet than honey-dew
Of all thy nights and days of ravishment,
Thy birds, thy cowslips and thy hawthorn's breath?

The empress of the year, the meadows' queen,
Back from the East, with all her goodly train,
Is come, to glorify the world again
With length of light and middle Summer-sheen.
In every plot, upon her throne of green,
Bright blooms the rose; with birds and blossom-rain
And perfume ecstasied are wood and plain
And Winter is as if it ne'er had been.
Oh June, liege lady of the flowering prime,
Now that thrush, finch, lark, linnet, ousel, wren
Thy praises pipe, to the Iranian bard
How shall we hearken, who, the highwaymen
Autumn and Winter, warns us, follow hard
On thy fair feet and bide their baleful time?

The meadows slumber in the golden shine;
Full-mirrored in the river's glass serene,
Stirless, the blue sky sleeps; knee-deep in green,

Nigh o'er-content for grazing are the kine.
The russet hops hang ripening on the bine;
The birds are mute; no clouds there are between
The slumbering lands to come and the sun's sheen;
The day is drowsed with Summer's wildering wine.
Peace over all is writ: fought is the fight;
From Winter for the nonce the field is won
And the tired earth can slumber in the sun
And dream her summer-dreams of still increase;
Whilst, as the long rays lengthen to the night,
The breeze o'er all the landscape murmurs "Peace!"

AUGUST

August, thou monarch of the mellow noon,
That with thy sceptre smit'st the teeming plain
And gladd'nest all the world with golden grain,
How oft have I, beneath thy harvest moon,
Hearkened the cushat's soft insistent croon,
As to the night she told her soul in pain,
Or heard the corn-crake to his mate complain,
When all things slept, beneath the sun aswoon!
The world with sun and sheen is overfed
And the faint heart, its need once done away,
Soon waxes weary of the summer-day
And the sun blazing in the blue o'erhead,
"Would God that it were night!" is apt to say
And "Would the summer-heats were oversped!"

SEPTEMBER

How is the world of Summer's splendours shorn!
The rose has had its day; from weald and wold
Past is the blossom-pomp, the harvest-gold;
The fields are orphaned of the ripened corn.
The meads, of their lush livery forlorn,
Lie bare and cheerless; Summer's tale is told
And Autumn reigns; the world is waxing old,
Its youth forspent in Plenty's heaped-up horn.
Yet, though the leaves, September, sere and brown
Show on thy time-awearied trees, in sign
Of life burned low, retreating to the root,
With jewels rich and rare, whose like no mine
On earth might yield, bound are thy brows for crown,

Purple and gold and red, of ripening fruit.

OCTOBER

October, May of the descending days,
Mid-Spring of Autumn, on the shortening stair
Of the year's eld abiding still and fair,
A pause of peace, when all the world at gaze,
'Neath the mild mirage of thy sun tilled haze,
Chewing the cud of Summer's sweets that were,
Lingers, unmindful of the Winter's care,
Yet in thy russet woods and leaf-strewn ways;
Sweet was the Summer, sweeter yet the Spring;
But in these mist attempered noons of thine,
Hung with the clustering jewels ol the vine,
And in thy ruddock's clear, contented lay,
A charm of solace is, that in no thing
To Summer suns may yield or blossoms gay.

NOVEMBER

The tale of wake is told; the stage is bare,
The curtain falls upon the ended play;
November's fogs arise, to hide away
The withered wrack of that which was so fair:
Summer is gone to be with things that were.
The sun is fallen from his ancient sway;
The night primaeval trenches on the day:
Without the Winter waits upon the stair.
Stern herald of the wintry wrath to come,
The mist-month treads upon October's feet,
Muting' the small birds' song, the insects' hum,
And all involving in its winding-sheet,
Graves on the frontal of the failing year,
"All hope abandon, ye who enter here!"

DECEMBER

The roofs are dreary with the drifted rime
And in the air a stillness as of death
Th'approach of some portentousness foresaith.
December comes, the tyrant of the time,

Vaunt-courier of the cold hybernal clime.
Mute is the world for misery; no breath
Nor stir of sound there is, that welcometh
The coming of the Winter's woeful prime.
"Alack! Was ever such a thing as Spring?"
We say, hand-holding to the hearths of Yule.
"Did ever roses blow or throstles sing?"
And in our ears the wild blast shrilleth; "Fool,
"That, in this world of ruin and decay,
"Thy heart's hopes buildedst on the Summer day!'

TWO DAYBREAKS

I. WINTER

The white light wakened me at morning-gray
And to the window in the dawn I went.
The dying night with the snow's sacrament
New houseled was and stark the white world lay
Under the grimness of the growing day,
Its wan face lifting to the firmament,
That, with its endless, ashen-coloured tent,
From pole to pole space vaulted, aye to aye.
Corpse of cold Nature, who might ever deem
That thou again from Winter's deathly dream
Shouldst wake, to wanton in the sunlight sweet
And see the lark wing skyward through the cloud,
Shouldst scent the roses in the Summer-heat
And hear the thrush among the leafage loud?

II. SPRING

The opal flush of dawn is in the sky;
Already m the limes I hear begun
The chirp of birds, awaking one by one;
And yonder in the East the lark mounts high,
Shrill-singing, looking, longing to espy
The rosy-footed heralds that fore run
The crimson standards of the coming sun:
Gone is the night, the golden day draws nigh.
Ah Spring, what winter shall fordo thy sweet?
How, in the sorry season of the snows,
Shall we forget thy silver sandalled feet,
Thai walked with us in April's primrose-way?

l low but remember that we smell the rose
And carolled in the cowslip meads ol May?

IN THE HALLERTHAL

(LUXEMBOURG)

The water wandered singing by my feet,
As through the dells, with many a red-boled beech
O'erarched, I went, that from the fiery reach
The wood ways warded of the noontide heat.
Through thronging ferns the silver stream did fleet,
Past range on range of temples, each on each
Ensuing still, without the tongue of speech
That told the story of a time effete.
Ah me, thou tiny, trotting, trickling thread,
Mid age-bleached rock and maze of living green
Thy little life that livest, never dead,
How many a generation hast thou seen!
How many an age hath come and gone, whilst thou
Thy careless ditty chantedst then as now!

PROPHETS OF THE PRIME

I. CROCUSES

But yesterday the world without was white;
And now the sap begins to stir anew.
The grass is starred with cups of gold and blue,
Lilac and silver, flakes of living light,
As of a rainbow fallen in the night.
The crocuses are up, a cheery crew:
Weary of tarrying the Winter through,
They might not wait till Spring for the sun's sight.
Vaunt-couriers of the world's awakening,
That quicken, in the middle Winter's woe,
Our hearts with your kaleidoscopic show,
Ye mind us of hope's seed in every thing,
How Winter wan there's none but hath its Spring,
Nor soul so sad but joy again may know.

II. HYACINTHS

What are these bright and glorious of array,
An army as with banners, risen to break
The Winter's rearward battle and to make
High proclamation in each garden-way
Of all the flowering witcheries of May,
Myriads of summer-thoughts that overtake
The land with sudden splendour and awake
The dumb wan world unto the morrowing day?
These are the visions of the slumbering earth,
Amiddleward the weary winter night,
Visions of sun and sheen and summer-mirth
Dreamt out aloud unto the lightening sky,
What time the world, ere yet the day wax white,
Dreams that she dreams and knows the waking nigh.

3. TULIPS

The tulips are abroad beneath the sun.
Like to a company of topers, fain,
After long drouth, the goblet full to drain,
O'er the brown earth, a-smile for winter done,
With lips uplifted to the light, they run,
Such draughts in-drinking of the golden rain,
Before the blithe day pass and summer wane.
There scarce would seem enough for ever)
What can be goodlier, tulips, or more sweet
Than this your life, that, for a blooming while,
Mower out and flourish in the full sun
Then, Summer over, to your bulbs retreat
And snugly their the Winter sleep away
Not wake to blossom till another May?

NATURE'S SECRET

I went in woodlands when the leaves were sere:
The watchet skies of Autumn, clear and cold,
Peeped through their panoplies of red and gold;
The wind went dirging to the dying year.
Yet in the wan waste ways a subtle cheer
There breathed; and as I sought to take and hold
The spell of peace that hallowed wood and wold,
"Content!" the robin carolled in mine ear.
Yea, all that is on earth's alike content

To die and in its like to live again,
Save man, that, after seventy years of pain
And strife, clings yet to personality
And wearies heaven with his vain lament
That others in his likeness live, not he.

IN WINTER

Methinks, in the dead season of the year,
The very nakedness of Nature brings
A keener sight into the soul of things,
The heart to Nature's heart become more near,
When 'gainst the sky the boughs are black and sere:
And to the eye, with leaves and blossomings,
With sky and sun undazed and flash of wings,
The general scheme of all seems grown more clear.
Nay, this I know; the spirit of delight
Far franklier stirs my heart to songful cheer
And my soul flowers in the Winter's night
More freely than when Spring by mead and mere
Leads her bright train or Summer to the height
Runs up the gamut of the flowering year.

FALSE FEBRUARY

Not seldom, whilst the Winter yet is king,
Whilst yet the meads are mute and boughs are bare,
A stirring in the February air
There comes, as with a faint foreshadowing,
A passing prophecy of far-off Spring
And distant days, when all the world shall wear
The lovely liveries of Summer fair,
That sets our wintry thought upon the wing.
Well though we know the thing's a Winter's trick.
To hold the soul with expectation sick,
And he will soon resume his iron reign,
Yet our fond hearts alone with hope in vain
Swell not; for hark, the swallows in the eaves
Rejoice as though the world were lush with leaves.

PRIMULA VERIS

I

I do remember whiles, when I have been
Walking, where March went roaring to his end.
In woods, with heart whose sadness did extend
To all I met and looked on, to have seen
A sudden primrose in the treefoot-green,
The which so bright on me did bend,
Meseemed that I had found some long-lost friend,
Whose aspect did away my winter's spleen.
There, in the rotting leaves, at the tree-foot,
Its wax-pure whorl of emerald pale it spread
And in corruption delving with its root,
The leaden heavens outfaced with lifted head
And infantile frank eyes, that seemed to me
The primal type ol taintless purity.

II

Sweet soul of the resuscitated earth,
That of the Springtide, tarrying yet afar,
In the bare wood-ways, with thy pure pale star,
Tellest and lightenest Life's night of dearth,
Few things as thou, meseems, are worship-worth,
That, when all creatures else with many a scar
And wound of Winter mute and stricken are,
Alone bear'st witness of the world's rebirth.
Soon shall the hyacinth outblazon thee
And daffodil and wood-anemone
Broider the ways with wealthier blossoming,
Cowslips and violets more perfume bring;
Yet, primrose, still beloved shalt thou be
O'er all, that art the morning-star of Spring.

THE HILLS WHENCE MY HELP COMETH

My thought still harbours where the silence fills
The far majestic mountains, as they reign,
Kings crowned with silver, o'er the subject plain.
Whether, rose-vestured, in the morning's sills
They stand or, with the sunset's flaming rills
Imperial purple clad, they glow or stain
With blue the distances of noon inane,
My heart is with the everlasting hills.
There, on those summits where the Immortals dwell,

With clouds and fires and thunders fenced about
'Gainst the profane, as he of Israel
That was the song-voice saith, still hope for me
Of help abideth and I look thereout
To have deliverance in days to be.

THE FIRST OF THE ALPS

The train fled, hurtling, through the summer-night,
Across the still flat plains of slumbering France,
And I, I waited, in a waking trance,
For that which was to come with Coming light:
And with the first faint streaks of morning-white,
The plains began, meseemed, to heave and dance
On either hand; it was the first advance
Of the hill-host that soared upon my sight.
Then, as the day drew on and light waxed wide,
The hills to mountains swelled on every side
And in the distance, like a giant ghost
Of the world's morning, 'gainst the sapphire sky,
The first fore-runner of the Titan host
Of the snow-summits hove and towered high.

SPRING-SADNESS

The middle-sweet of Spring is come
And everywhere the thorn is gray:
The world has put its woes away,
Forgot its Winter's martyrdom:
The cuckoo, in the noon-tide hum,
Answers the throstle on the spray.
My heart is heedless of the May;
The throstle in my throat is dumb.
What ails thee, heart? But yesternight
It seems, when all the world was white,
The seeds of 50ng in thee did spring
And ripened up to flower and fruit;
And now, when all with blossoming
And pipe of birds is glad, thou'rt mute!

THE LARK

"The sun is up and up with it am I!"
Thus, in a rain of golden melody,
From th'empyrean wafted 'twas to me,
And in the topmost blue I might espy
The lark upmounting higher and more high,
As, with his pinions spurning land and sea,
Still singing, winging, sun-ward travelled he,
As if new heavens he sought beyond the sky.
Voice of the world's aspiring, as our soul
Thou art, that with no earthly heaven or sun
Contented is, but for its wish unwon
Upstraineth still beyond the topmost pole,
To where all wishes solved, all wills made one
Are in the effulgence of the Undifferenced Whole.

VER SALUTIFERUM

The throstles wakened me at morning-red
With such a wild melodious choral shout
Of songful jubilance, I might not doubt
But Spring at last was come and Winter sped.
And of a truth it was as they had said;
For all the world with radiance new about
Was raimented and in me, as without,
Delight there stirred that long had lain for dead.
For who was ever yet might still be sad,
When all the world for Winter gone is glad
And who, when all things bud and bloom and sing,
But in the rathe sweet season had relief
Of pain and offered up his Winter's grief
Upon the Mower-bound altars of the Spring?

ROSA BENEDICTA

Was ever wonder rarer than the rose.
That, with its gala-robes of green and red,
In the mid-prime uprears its regal head,
Hailing us glory in the winter's woes
Bygone and summer come in garden-close
And meadow wide? With breath of balsam shed,
It mindeth us that beauty is not dead
And Love for lovers lives, if but for those.
Small marvel if with us brief space it bide,
If, of its heaven's eternal blossom-tide

Remembering it, beneath our grey sky-dome,
In this our world of winter and lament,
It weary after its celestial home
And pine and pass for very languishment!

THE DEATH OF THE WOOD-WARBLER

I read to-day how one, who loved birds well,
Lit erst upon a little wild wood wren,
That, old and solitary, in a glen
Among the trees beside a spring did dwell;
How friendship betwixt man and bird befell,
Till it, at last, its tear forgot of men.
Slept on his hand, contented, and how then
He found it later dead beside the well.
Ah, what a homily to humankind
This preacheth, that had been joy's very spright
And old and lonely grown, no whit repined
For pleasant life fordone and day lall'n night,
But poetlike, 'spite age and solitude.
Piped on till death, m cheer and courage good!

LILIES

This middle summer morn, an angel band,
Meseems, is lighted down upon the sward;
In robes of light arrayed, with torch and sword,
The airs of heaven they breathe on every hand.
It is the lilies, in the grass that stand
And o'er the July-prime keep watch and ward,
Telling, with bells of frozen snow, fire-cored,
Sweet Summer's triumph to the laughing land.
Who would not, lilies, deem your lovely light
O'er sweet to pass and like the prime, too fair
For Death's unlovesome manage that you were?
Yet must you die and day give place to night;
For all that is must have its wax and wane
And all that's fair must fade, to flower again.

FEATHERED INGRATES

In the March-morning all the world was bright:

The thrushes and the blackbirds on the lawn
Were busy ere the dark was wholly gone.
There was their table spread from overnight
With crumbs and all a songbird's appetite
Might tempt: but thicker, there, than mushroom-spawn,
Alack! were crocuses, as flush of dawn
Purple and golden, lilac, blue and white.
What ailed you, feathered rogues, to make your prey
Of these frail firstlings of the flowered year
And mar their vernal pomp, in mischief pure,
Churl-fashion? Manlike, more than bird-like, sure,
'Twas thus my hospitality to pay
My lawn by spoiling of its Springtide cheer.

CONVALLARIA MAJALIS

I am the Lily of the Valley.
Where in the woods the silence dwells,
My tiny spire of silver bells
I rear in every verdant alley,
That, to the dance when elves did sally
Anights, with chimings filled the dells:
But, now, within its silver cells
The music's mute, past power to rally.
Yet in my soul the song-pulse tarries
And from its proper port of sound
Debarred, to other senses marries
Itself; and so, where May is found,
The wild wood breeze in perfume carries
My heart's dumb yearning all around.

A MID-MARCH DAY

My heart is heavy on this mid-March day,
When from the mouth of hell the East Wind blows,
With menace of immeasurable woes
Winnowing the air. Though Spring is on the way
And with its promise of the middle May
In the rathe beds die tulip-flame foreshows
The tale of coming summer and the rose,
The time is sadder than the Winter grey.
Dead season of the snows, is't not enough
That thou shouldst fetter us for half the year
In chains of frost, but with thy counterbuff

Of blood-encurdling blasts our infant Spring
Thou thus must poison and thy phantom drear
'T'wixt us intrude and Life's requickening?

AUTUMN

Gone are the Gods; the time for new is near:
Past is the Summer, past the harvesting:
The meads are mute; the birds have ceased to sing;
Dim is the sun, that yesterday was clear,
And gray the heavens dull-mirrored in the mere.
Yet in the woods the leaves' emblazoning
Outglories all the gladness of the Spring,
Decking the last days of the labouring year.
How comes it, these, of all things new and old,
Alone do glory in their own decay
And garb themselves to die in red and gold,
As if with stress of good and evil chance
Forwearied and content to pass away,
Accounting death to be deliverance?

TWO RIVERS

I. NILUS

Mother of waters, how shalt thou abide
Man's inquest? Calm, unfathomable, broad,
Thou wanderest from the solitudes untrod,
A half-world measuring with majestic tide,
Whose march nor day nor night hath e'er awried,
Whilst, nation after nation, at Fate's nod,
Hath past and God succeeded unto God
And aeon after aeon risen and died.
Laden with immemorial memories,
Mysterious, mute, with fertilising hands,
That scatter benison upon the lands
And clothe the wastes with harvests and with trees,
Thou lapsest through the immeasurable sands,
To lose thyself in the eternal seas.

II. THAMESIS

How shall I do thee honour, homely Thames,
That, on thy silent breast of sober brown,
Unto the mid-heart of the teeming town
The world's wealth bring'st, in many a fleet that stems
Thy waters, garnering in thy garment's hems
The treasures of the East and West, laid down
Our England's brows to circle with a crown
Of harvests more of price than gold and gems?
Thou art not fair, save to the spirit's eyes;
Yet, in thy constancy of duty done
And undespairing labour, reckoning none
That makes of frowning or of smiling skies,
For me a spiritual beauty lies,
That is beyond the lapse of stars and sun.

II.

THE NIGHT-WATCHES

WHITE NIGHTS

I

How have I sinned against thy statutes. Sleep,
That thou this many a year forsaken hast
My sorry eyes, that, whilst, their cares offcast.
All else are sunken in thy drowsy deep.
I, only I, the weapon-watch must keep,
Revolving still in thought the piteous Past,
The laggard hours each heavier than the last.
Till the chill dawn in at my casements peep?
Oh, for an hour of antick Thessaly,
That I might steep me, with Medean spells,
Mandragora and heavy hæmony
And what herb else the assaining God compels.
The cup that sets the imprisoned spirit free
At will to wander in the dreamland's dells!

II

"Let me but perish in the face of light!"
So spake the ancient Greek, and so say I.
How many a time, with dimmed and haggard eye
Following the dull hours in their halting flight
Along the aisles of never-ending night,

Old Ajax' prayer I've prayed, with many a sigh,
As one condemned, who longs, before lie die.
To look once more upon the morning white!
Nay, in the dreary fever-dreams of wake
Not seldom I, despairing oi the Lark,
Deem that the blue day never more shall break
Nor morning glimmer white nor henceforth reign
But the blind twins of blank disfeaturing dark
And fore eternal Chaos come again.

III

In my young days, for sleep I did not wait,
But, rising up, when all the world slept sweet,
Followed the flying foe through square and street.
Oft over hill and stream the dim white day
Wax have I watched to radiance, ray by ray,
And seen the glistering morn, with golden feet
Chasing the shadows from their each retreat,
Awake and glorify the city gray.
But now that with the years the youthful heat
No more runs riot in each pulse and vein
And the fierce fires, that in the blood had seat,
For refuge now have gotten them to the brain,
My feet are still and thought for them and me
The wander-staff must wield by land and sea.

IV

Love grows by longing, so the poets tell:
And if, indeed, the saw not always sooth
Be of the fitful loves of fickle youth,
With age's wistfulness it fitteth well.
And of all longings which the soul compel,
That which the sleepless harbour for the ruth
Of kindly slumber sharpest is of tooth
And worst of woes which were since Adam fell.
Yet, if wont wax by what it battens on
And want by that whereon it fain would feed,
Methinketh, an eternity or two
From my tired eyes and my strained sense 'twill need
The dust of wakefulness away to do
With the sweet waters of oblivion.

DREAM-MEETINGS

Whiles, in the midnight hours, upon my bed,
In dreams once more to me the old delight
Returns and in the visions of the night,
I look upon the faces of my dead.
No thought there is of sorrow, no tears shed.
No word of woe, but unto touch and sight
All is as once it was, the eyes as bright,
The hands as living warm, the Lips as red.
But, in the morn, my dreams when I retrace,
Remembrance rends me of the Might-have-been
And to the house of grief I set my face,
Nay, were, methinks, less sad, if I had seen
The dear-loved dead, in all sleep's marble sheen,
Lie with closed lids the coffin-boards between.

THE CUSHAT

The wind was wailing in the trees all night,
Before my sills, but in the middle noon
Of night there came the mild mysterious moon,
And with the wonder of her silver sight,
The dim gray world was gladdened and waxed white;
The shrill winds slackened from their wailing tune
And left uprise the soft complaining croon
Of some stray cushat on the limes alight.
Poor pilgrim, from the Summer woods astray,
What old commandment of unfavouring Fate
Drove thee from thy warm lodging in the green,
With my dull heart to mourn thy hopes' dismay,
In the gray town, where sad are small and great
And pine for air and sunlight, like the treen?

ANIMAE VIGILIUM

Whenas the spirit's vigil,'in clear dream
And solemn vision shrined, anights I keep,
What while the world is sanctified with sleep,
Thought, over all the troubled, surging stream
Of darkling life casting its searching beam,
Bids, with its ruthless radiance, from the deep
Into full light the things eternal leap
And strips from those the splendour which but seem.

Then many a thing, which in men's sight is good
And fair, unblest and foul to us is shown
And many a God and many a Holy Rood
In that dread hour resolves to wood and stone;
Nay, when the sun returneth with the day,
Meseems that light with night hath past away.

THE FOREDAWN HOUR

I

Between the night-end and the break of day
An hour there is that from the thither shore
Of the dark river its enchantments frore
And fearful borrows, when each churchyard-clay
Breathes out its chills, when life unto a stay
Seems come and pauses, shuddering, at Death's door,
That stands ajar; of all the twenty-four
Sternest and most of horror and affray.
Here, for arraignment, all its sour and sweet,
Its crimes, its wrongs, its errors, its tears shed,
(For sorrows here for sins imputed are)
The piteous Past unto Thought's judgment-bar
Brings up; and here, where night and morning meet,
The sea of memory gives up its dead.

II

Here, all alone, the soul before the ark
(That ark whereto there is no mercy-seat)
Of conscience stands and to the iron beat
Of time, that all the wasted years doth mark
And all the days in vain bygone, must hark,
Mourning for done and undone, deeds unmeet
And words ill-spoken; whilst, with faltering feet,
The night slopes dawnward through the shallowing dark.
Set, awful hour, when, in the grave-cold air,
The moments fall like ages, when Life's breath
Halts and the world lies blank and stark and bare
Before thought's eyes, when love and life and light
For ever sunken seem in seas of night
And the soul pauses in the ports of Death.

III

Who to this dread diurnal judgment-hour,
This everyday rehearsal-time of death,
When life stands still and cold is Nature's breath.
When all our sins bygone like mountains tower
Before the thought and with its salving power,
Alar the blessed daylight tarrieth, —
Who is't can look with hope and cheer and faith?
Who hut before its cold approach must cower?
Then for a God, with blind hand, round about
Casting, to succour it and finding none,
The soul into the darkness crieth out
For some twin soul, to share its hope and doubt.
And meeting but the void, till night be done.
Longeth and trembleth tor the assaining sun.

IV

Oft, in this darkling hour of doubt and dread,
The Past, with all its ghosts, revisits me,
Its wraiths of hope and joy and ecstasy:
I feel the windy presence of the dead
Stir in my hair and hear their spirit-tread,
As dry leaves falling, nothing though I see:
Again for my sad sense they live and be
And stir and rustle round about my bed.
Oh spirits of my dead, that may not rest,
But needs must harbour where you loved of yore,
Still, by the fetters of the grave opprest,
Seeking to burst the bonds of nothingness,
How shall I do to ease you of your stress?
How shall I win to look on you once more?

RETROSPECT

Whenas the Past unto the stern assize
Of middle night I summon and survey,
With backward thought, the over-travelled way,
Much for repentance, yea, and much for sighs
And more for shamefast sorrow, to mine eyes
There doth appear, and needs my head away
Turn must I from the record for dismay
Which graven there in fire eternal lies.
But for a solace yet I have the thought,

That none I willingly did ever wrong;
And much, meseems, for duty hath he wrought
Who ne'er the eternal things hath sold or bought
And with his unsophisticated song,
The healing tears to some sad eyes hath brought.

TO THE BELOVED DEAD

I call upon you "in the collied night,"
When all things sleep and only I, I wake,
Beseeching you to come for pity's sake
And my sad eyes to solace with your sight.
How many a time I've watched the dark grow white,
Expecting still to see the shadow take
Your shape, to hear your voice the silence break,
Your speech renew for me the dead delight!
I will not question you. I will not weep;
I will not seek to strain you to my breast:
Let me but look upon your face in sleep,
But feel your touch, but hear you voice my name,
And you shall go, returning whence you came,
And have again your cold and senseless rest.

III.

MUSICALIA

BUT FOR MUSIC

"Were music not, in this our world, well nigh
"Might we avouch, the Beautiful is dead".
So it of one who knew life well! was said,
Beauty of that which to the ear and eye
Immediate is, which to the sense speaks high,
Intending. Here for how were beauty bred,
Where all fore-ordered is by count of head
Of brute majorities, but born to die?
Wherefore, thou darling spirit of delight,
That to our souls, with toil and misery
Forwearied, speak'st of lands of love and light,
Of isles of rest beyond the sheer sun's sight,
Whereas new heavens new earth o'erarch and sea,
Blessed be thou to all eternity!

HAYDN

As on one walking in the graves by night
The glad May morning comes at unawares
And the young day, with all its frolic airs
And throstles' song and scent and flower-delight,
Brims up his darkling soul with life and light,
So, in our time, when vain Tchaikowskj tears
Our still-vexed ears and dreary Dvorak shares
With Brahms and Sullivan the dullard might,
Haydn, thine unsophisticated strain.
Wherein the fields flower and the small birds sing,
Our saddened souls to life and love again
Restores and sets our laggard thought a wing
To where May memories fill the heart's inane
With all the happy auspices of Spring.

SCHUBERT

Death, weary grown of monody and dirge,
A singer sought to fill his funeral halls
With strains of jubilation, such as Saul's
Dark spirit in its frenzied hour did purge,
And hearing from afar thy golden surge,
Schubert, of song, straight from earth's echoing walls
He bore thee off, with all its swells and falls,
The tide of tune for him thenceforth to urge.
Surely, such strains as thine might never die,
But, here though mute, must otherwhere throb high:
Surely, in heaven above thou dost prolong
The measures of thine unaccomplished song
And heark'nest, in some interstellar land,
The sphere-harp answer to thy pulsing hand.

MENDELSSOHN

This of the children of the bride-chamber
Was, sure, who mourn not, for the bridegroom yet
With them abideth. Pure of passion's fret,
His song the springs of love and peace doth stir,
Brimming with bliss unmingled heart and ear,
As of the harps before the White Throne set,

That, with their golden jubilance, unlet
Of time, hymn on in heaven's eternal year.
Whilst in this weary world yet hearts there be,
Which forth unto sweet music fain must go,
Still shall his glory fill the lands, though he,
From fret of life and death delivered long,
The rapturous tides of heaven ebb and flow
Feeleth and hearkeneth to the angels' song.

BERLIOZ

What didst thou here, proud spirit, sad and stern,
In this stepmother world, where praise and fame
But seldom wait upon his living name
Whose high-plumed soul the accustomed ways doth spurn?
To thee alive thy France deaf ears did turn
And now, when all the world doth thee acclaim,
Waking too late to her undying shame,
Vain offerings pours upon thy funeral urn.
Ah would the Gods beyond the grave may some
Requital for thy life's long martyrdom
Foreordered have! May Shakspeare's mighty spright
With Byron, Virgil, Goethe there unite
With love to welcome thee and thanks and praise
And bind thy brows with sempervernal bays!

LISZT

I. CONCERTO IN E

Where art thou, art thou, King of Faerie?
These be thy golden woods, where human foot
Befalleth not nor noise of hounds nor bruit
Of bugle echoing from tree to tree;
No mortal thing is there to hear or see;
Only thine ivory horn and Robin's flute,
Mab's silver psaltery and Titania's lute,
Answer m) call with elfin minstrel
And lo! what splendours shimmer through the green?
Here be the revels of the fairy queen.
Yonder she fareth on her milkwhite steed
And in her train, with many a pipe and reed,
The elf-rout sweeps the jewelled glade along,
Fluttering the silence with a fairy song.

II. CONCERTO IN A

Where hast thou hearkened to these strains, my soul?
Sure, in some realm beyond the stars it must
Have been, some land where love is free from lust,
Some plane of peace above the topmost pole,
Where, quit of hope and passion, joy and dole,
The unfettered spirit, not yet set to rust
And wither in this raiment of the dust,
Resteth serene upon the Eternal Whole.
There, cradled on the Present's golden shore,
No Past behind it, no To-be before,
From love and memory and doubt and strife
Absolved, it meditates the things that are,
Or e'er it leave its own particular star
And launch anew upon the storms of life.

III. CONSOLATION IN E

Love comes to us at morning,
With hands fulfilled of flowers,
Youth's path with sun and showers
He fareth still adorning;
But, when the West gives warning
Of night and Life's sky lowers
Toward the evening hours,
He flees from us with scorning.
Yet in his room he leaveth,
For those who serve him well,
One who more often grieveth
Thou joyeth, but whose spell
Salveth Love's loss's shame:
Affection is his name.

IV. LIEBESTRAUM

Medreamt I saw Love like a lute player
Come carolling to me along the stream.
Bound were his temples with the gla'd sun's beam
And in his hand he held a dulcimer,
Among whose strings a little wind did stir.

And "Do I wake", to him I said, "or dream?
"And dost thou live, indeed, or only seem?
"Long have I lacked thee, many a weary year."
But he, "Away! I come not now for thee.
"What would you rhymesters with my golden boon,
"Who all things twist into an idle tune?
"Forsooth, for those alone my favours be,
"Who in this round do nothing but my will
"And without thought the world's desire fulfil."

GLANES DE WORONINCE, N°. 3

The wind about the mountain wandered sighing;
The autumn day with showers was sad and chill;
No light from heaven there fell on field and rill,
Save some faint gold-streaks on the cloud-line lying,
Where in the Western sky the da) was dying:
And in the ways that circled round the hill
I wandered straying at the wild wind's will.
My soul for sadness with its sadness vying.
But, as I came unto the topmost mountain,
Out from tin' cloudwrack sudden burst the sun
And all the landscape with their flooding fountain
Of rosy gold his rays did overrun;
And a voice whispered me, "A truce to sorrow!
"Belike, the sun shall shine again to-morrow."

6. DIVINA COMMEDIA SYMPHONY

Andante con moto quasi Allegretto

This is the purging-place for things ill-done
And things left undone. In the twilit air
Of dawn, I mount Eld's purgatorial stair,
Whilst all about my way thought's fires there run,
Wherein Life's absolution must be won:
And at the hill-foot, upward as I fare,
For sign of hope and charm against despair,
The waters tremble in the waxing sun.
Here be no pangs of hell; no fiends affright
Our Constance, as we urge our pilgrim way,
With eyes uplifted to the morrowing day;
Only the fining-fires of age contrite,
That, with their purging, purifying breath,

Befit us for the sacrament of death.

REVE IN E (AU SALON)

All night through the dance and its mazes we swayed:
The folk murmured round us, I knew not of what;
A dream was upon me; I heeded them not,
As I lay in the arms of that loveliest maid.
The wind of the night in her tresses there played;
The stars through the casements their rays on us shot,
As we danced on together, the world all forgot,
To the music the flutes and the violins made.
Through orange-groves gleaming with flowerage and fruit
We floated, we twain, whilst, around and above,
The horn-notes, that blent with the voice of the flute,
Still mimicked the moan of the murmurous dove.
Had the flute-notes not failed and the horns fallen mute,
We had danced on for ever, myself and my love.

I. SIEGLINDE

Alack, Sieglinde, whither wilt thou flee?
All things conspire against thee, old and new;
Fire, earth, air, water, all will thee undo.
Why wast thou born, fair maid? Ah, woe is me!
For in thy footsteps, over land and sea,
Wherever earth is green and heaven blue,
Fate and the hour, relentless, still pursue:
There is no room in this wide world for thee.
Nor yet, in all, thy death, sad loveling, may
The vengeance of the Gods supernal sate
And the red maw of unrelenting Fate.
Quick art thou with a seed, which, day by d
Unto a flower of hate and grief shall grow
And whelm the heavens and the earth with woe.

II. WOTAN

"Remote, unfriended, melancholy, slow!"
Such are the names, o eldest of the Gods,
That on thy head they heap, the crackbrain clods,
For whom Francesca and her Paolo
Are but an idle tale of long ago,
For whom Orestes with the Furies' rods
Anil pale Prometheus on his rock at odds
With the fierce Fates are but a passing show.
Heed thou them not; tiny fool their hour and go
Some little fulsome honey filched from life,
Back to their hell. Hut we, who love and know
That which it is to suffer evenso,
Look with wet eyes upon thy luckless strife
And our hearts throb in answer to thy woe.

III. BRÜNNHILDE

Lady of Sorrows, sore of Love's wild will
Undone, of love, indeed, transformed to hate,
Yet love enough abiding with thy mate
Thee, that didst slay him, in his death to kill,
How wilt thou do? Walhalla's burnings fill
The heavens inane with smoke: in Asgard's gate
Wotan thy sire lies fall'n, the wise, the great;
And the Gods' Twilight holds Gladheimr hill.
Where wilt thou flee? Yet, though thy heavenly place
No longer wait thee, thou, from Siegfried's pyre
With him ascending on the wings of fire
To heaven, Walhalla with a tripled grace
Shalt find rebuilt and with thy hero stand
By Balder in the new immortal band.

IV. HAGEN

"Grown old before my time, the glad I hate",
Quoth haughty Hagen. I, that, hating none,
Still in my heart Love harbour, as a sun,
The winterward of life that doth abate,
And do but scorn the glad, the fools of Fate,
I cannot yet but hail thee, dreadful son
Of Night and Hell, unconquerable one,
In sin and shame that yet art grimly great.
Stern fallen Angel of the old Norse day,
Thou, as the Satan of our latter lay,

The protest 'gainst triumphant dulness art
And brute o'erweening force of the world's heart,
That, when our Siegfrieds wax intolerable,
Some Hagen sends to hurl them down to hell.

V. ISOLDE

Alone, Isolde, is thy hero fled
Unto the wild and darkling wastes of death,
Whose road no traveller retravelleth,'
To tell the tale of how he there hath sped;
Nor spared his henchman to the place of dread
With him to carry where he journeyeth;
Yet thee, his bride, awaited not a breath,
That thou mightst follow him among the dead.
How in Death's incommensurable halls
Wilt thou discover where he doth abide?
How wilt thou win to come unto his side?
"Love to love, spirit unto spirit calls;
"And I, forbidden though to see his face,
"Shall spend Eternity in his embrace".

THE PEDIGREE OF THE ROMANTIC SCHOOL IN MUSIC

Haydn, thy hand 'twas first from heaven that brought
Promethean tire, fair music's failing light
Anew to kindle. From thy slackening might
The falling torch of song sweet Schubert caught
And bore it onward with the speed of thought,
Brightlier forever burning and more bright,
Till all too soon, for Time's untimeous spite,
lie too must pass and leave his work half-wrought,
Then Berlioz took the fiery cross again
And bore it flaming over land and sea,
'Spite dearth and doubt and scorn, triumphantly,
Till to his succour other champions twain,
Wagner and Liszt, there came: and who were fain
to add a fourth unto these Thunderers three?

MENDELSSOHN.

I. QUARTETT OP. 12 IN E

What are these wild sweet voices, swelling, thronging
About the wood-ways, with the frolic beams
Of fancy oversunned, wherein, meseems,
Shy Nature's very speech I hear prolonging
A tale of realms of rapture, from Life's wronging
Removed afar, of Paradisal dreams,
Dreamt out by undiscovered meads and streams,
That overfloods my soul with love and longing?
Nought is there here of the affright and sadness
Which haunt the traces of our toiling feet;
But here the primal innocence and sweet
Of life abide, in all content and gladness,
Nor consolation from the hope need borrow
Of some imaginary better morrow.

II. A MINOR SYMPHONY. — ADAGIO.

All hail, thou holy, heaven-attempered soul,
That, hither banished from thy native sky
And in our dust-heap doomed to live and die,
Unstirred by all its chances, joy and dole,
With eyes fast fixed upon the constant pole,
Through all Life's shifting scenes, smile, tear, frown, sigh,
Earth's blandishments disdained, her lures put by,
Farest unfaltering tow'rd thy heavenly goal!
Now, happy spright, is thy release at hand;
Well nigh thy weary pilgrimage is o'er:
For, hark, the harps and flutes of heaven resound,
To welcome thee; its airs and flames around
Breathing, the angels hover, to the shore
To bear thee of the blue celestial land.

MERKEL

MAILIED, OP. 18, N°. I

Ten o'clock of a morn of May!
The air wells over with wilding rhyme;
The throstle trills on the leafing lime:
"The nest is built on the bending spray;
"The eggs are hatching"; I hear him say.
"The summer cometh! With song 'tis time
"To hail the heart of the pleasant prime,

"The mid-Spring sweet of the dainty day."
Come, throstle, trill me thy sweetest song!
God wot, we have languished over long
For Winter-weariness, thou and I!
Our best and brightest behoveth sing,
Whilst green the grass is and blue the sky;
Alack! tor Summer is swift of wing.

LA COURSE À L'ABÎME

(BERLIOZ'S FAUST)

Meseems, the World-Faust, through the ages' night,
Upon the courier of the Will-to-be,
Hurtling across Life's darkling plains I see.
Deaf are his ears and blinded is his sight;
He turneth not aside to left or right;
Nay, through the shadows and the darkness, he.
The Mephistophiles Democracy
Spurring, ensueth still his headlong flight.
He noteth not the spectres of the Past
That on his cither hand for warning rise
He heedeth not the snakes "I doom that hiss
About him nor the portents in the skies;
But, at the demon's instance, hard and fast,
Urgeth, unchecked, his course to the abyss.

SCHUBERT

SYMPHONY IN C MAJOR

I. ANDANTE — ALLEGRO

Whence come these golden horn-notes, waning, swelling,
The soul with memories of the Past that stir?
From India's hills and Scythia's deserts drear
Afar they come, of ancient peoples telling,
Beyond the Oxus and the Indus dwelling,
And of the Wander-Lust, from year to year
In them that waxed, until it grew a spur,
Their feet into the wander-ways compelling.
Of impulse old they tell and ancient longing,
Unknowing that whereafter it did yearn,
Of vague strange fancies on the spirit thronging,

Of wishes wild that in the breast did burn,
Till all the thought became a wandering fire,
That needs must up and after its desire.

II. ANDANTE CON MOTO

The hautboys of the stir of preparation
Tell, of the gathering of the caravan,
Of the departure, man ensuing man,
Horde after horde and nation after nation,
Till all the deserts, station unto station,
With tribe on tribe are filled and clan on clan,
The rear belike a year behind the van,
All pouring Europe-ward without cessation.
Onward they press, of obstacles uncounting,
Hills over-climbing, crossing stream and sea,
Armies out-warring, battlements affronting,
Restless, resistless as fatality,
Till, with a final flux, the Alps surmounting,
They overflood the plains of Italy.

III. ALLEGRO VIVACE

Down-lapsing from the hills, a human ocean,
With shining arms and standards topped for foam,
To the sheer heart the torrent surges home
Of the old world: nor courage nor devotion
Nor wit can stay its Fate-foreordered motion.
No hope for her beneath the blue sky-dome,
At the barbarians' hands Imperial Rome,
Like Hannibal, must drink the deathly potion.
To their sphinx Asia used, where nothing alters,
Drunk with the wine of change they are: behold,
How of queens' necklets they their horses' halters
Make and kings' crowns cast in the pot for gold,
Their weapon-dance about the ruined altars
Of either faith wild urging, new and old.

IV. ALLEGRO FINALE

The stress is over, done the work of rending
Present from Past and soul from body free;
Accomplished is the appointed surgery,

That must avail the rotten Past for ending.
Now, with its healing salves, intent on mending
Life's bleeding wounds, from War's subsiding sea
Peace lifts its head and to the fair To-be
All things which live and are again are tending.
The world-leach Time, the Vssainei and Forgiver,
War's breaches heals in town and plain and mart;
From every quarter How Life's streams—as dart
On dart poured out they were from Natures quiver,
—Together, as a mighty, placid river,
Tow'rd the rebirth of the old world in Art.

AT THE PIANO

As o'er the answering keys my fingers stray,
The fluctuant fancies into music wooing
And through the haunts of harmony pursuing
The memories of many a bygone day,
The curtain of the Present drawn away
Is from my thought and with the veil's undoing,
The dear dead Past arises, the renewing
Seeking of that which moulders in the clay.
The loves of old once more I see resurging,
That long have slept beside the mouldered hates;
The olden joys and woes the dreamland's gates
Give up again and I, as o'er the abyss
Of thought I lean and watch the wraiths emerging,
Feel on my lips once more my first love's kiss.

FIELD'S NOCTURN, N°. 16 IN F

The larks are up, abroad in heaven outflinging
Their gladsome cadences of golden rhyme;
Upon the ground bass of the cuckoo's chime
The wrens make descant; all the woods are ringing
With the glad noise of thrush and linnet bringing
Their happy homage to the pleasant prime:
It is the early sweet of Summer-time
And all the air is full of scent and singing.
But hark! Whence comes that minor cadence, breaking
The sweet concent of happy harmony,
As of some moaning surf, sad music making
Upon the beach-bend of a sullen sea?
It is the thought of loves laid waste, awaking

The surges of the sea of memory.

ANDANTINO SOSTENUTO IN B

Sleep, sleep, sad memories, and in your sleep
Be woven all into a dulcet dream.
Wherein, regenerate by the salving stream
Of fain forgetfulness, your sense shall steep
In that afar unfathomable deep
Of peace, that lies beyond the sunset-gleam
And on its bosom bears the Hesperian beam
To lands of rest, where hope in heaven shall reap.
Look through the painted pane of Time's effacement,
Life's sweets remembering and its sours forgetting,
And fill my soul with light of consolation,
Even as the sunlight of a stormful setting
Shines through some many-hued cathedral casement,
O'erflooding all with Faith's transfiguration.

VALLÉE D'OBERMANN.

(A VERSE-TRANSCRIPTION OF LISZT'S TONE-POEM)

I.

I wander o'er the hills in lonely leisure;
Returning ever to the ancient ground,
Thought in my head still runs its endless round.
That which I prized of old no more I treasure;
In that which once I loved I have no pleasure:
Though still unchanged to touch and sight and sound.
In all I find no more what once 1 found;
Life's goods and ills I mete by other measure.
Since that for us, alas! the loss is certain,.
Since no unthinkable enchanted goal
For us there waits behind the future's curtain,
Such as might render to our shipwrecked soul
That which lost life from us hath year by year ta'en,
What for the loss shall of a world console?

II.

The tempest in my soul hath long subsided;
The winds have fallen calm, the waves are still;
Yet no sun comes hope's auspice to fulfil.
The light by which my spirit's bark I guided,
In whose direction I of old confided,
Whereby my way to steer 'twixt good and ill,
Is blotted out, nor aught for ever will
The hopes renew whereon I once abided.
No faith is left me in the olden story,
Which once my heart sufficed in every thing.
The light is faded from its golden glory;
Its holy memories have taken wing,
To their long home gone back in limbos hoary:
Doubt in the darkened soul of me is king.

III.

Much have I wrought, yet nought with me remaineth;
Long have I sought, yet nothing have in hand;
Far have I fared, yet never came to land.
How shall I do, whilst yet Life's light obtaineth,
The shores to reach where peace primaeval reigneth,
As in some sea-pool on a summer-strand,
Through whose bright waters, on the golden sand,
A fairy scape of seaflowers waxeth, waneth?
Not one am I that from the Past can borrow,
To gild to-day, the light of days fordone,
Nor on some fair fallacious golden morrow
False faith can stablish: nay, I am as one
Yet living buried in a grave of sorrow,
Who seeks no more to look upon the sun.

IV.

When Life's account I reckon, gains and losses,
It sickens me its unrequited slain
To count and see how many Christs in vain
Through this our changeless world have borne their crosses,
How many fighters perished in Life's fosses,
Whilst, with the old indifferent disdain,
Mankind upon its waves of strife and pain
From peak to peak the world-storm's torrent tosses.
Yet, as those bred and born in wars and slaughters
That sleep their dreamless sleep through fire and fight.
My consolation is that Lethe's waters

Have not yet lost their salutary might
The foolish hearts of Adam's sons and daughters
To solace with oblivion's dulcet night.

V.

Once consolation did I seek from Nature
For my sick soul: but now, alas! I know
That she no sympathy with man ran show.
Heeds not his glee nor his distemperature,
But, from the cold heights of her Titan stature,
Indifferent down upon his joy and woe
Looks, as upon the plains that spread below
The snow-peaks gaze, with faces blank of feature.
Yet, in her summer woods, her wastes hybernal,
Quit is the spirit of men's idle prate:
In her snow-death, in her renascence vernal,
With the world's soul it holds communion strait
td hears the throbbing pulse- of Time eternal
Measure the man lies of foreordered Fate.

VI.

Since thought as Life is, fleeting as the wind,
What booteth it to drive one's barren furrow
Through the dumb Past or in Time's grave to burrow
For that which none this side of death to find
May hope? What saith the wisest of our kind,
"Increase of knowledge brings increase of sorrow;
"Availeth not thought-taking for the morrow;
"Unto much wisdom is much grief assigned".
Since all must perish for the All's renewing,
Why waste for ever on thought's sterile fire?
Hearken no more to hope's fallacious wooing;
Cast stress and passion on life's funeral pyre.
This only thing on earth is worth th'ensuing,
Deliverance from the bondage of desire.

VII.

Could we but look, indeed, in coming ages
New hope in a new world of things to find,
Yet might we live, to this our day resigned.
Alas! in all the Past's recurrent stages,
In every word of poets, prophets, sages,

We read the changeless future of our kind,
What lies before us that which is behind,
The Past rewritten in the Present's pages.
Only the thought that life is not for ever,
That at the last a time shall come to free
Our hearts and brains from sterile thought's endeavour
And hopeless hope, some solace hath for me.
Hiding my face in thine all-sheltering Never,
Eternity, be thou my sanctuary!

IV

LITTERALIA

DANTE

When I of poets dream, not Spenser sweet
Nor Hafiz high it is that holds my thought;
Nor Shakspeare, last for crowning wonder wrought;
Nay, in my mind I see Ravenna street
And there, head bowed beneath the noontide heat,
A black-robed dreamer fare, austere and haught,
With eyes turned inward, unregarding aught,
Who no man greeteth and whom none doth greet:
And as he goes, at him the passers-by
Point with scared looks and murmur, "This is he
"Who did hell-fire and purging pains aby.
"Mark but how black his cheeks and temples be!"
Fools, see ye not upon his brows hell's stress
Not only writ, but Heaven's approof no less?

SPENSER

Spenser, thou first inspirer of my song.
That o'er the hills and meads of Arcady
Thy radiant train of ladies sweet to see
And mail-clad knights the woodways lead'st along,
The eternal laws of honour, right and wrong
Still hymning, who is there can vie with thee
For dear delight and frolic fantasy
Others in sterner measures and more strong
Of heaven and hell have sung and to a height
O'ervaulting thine have stopped the tuneful reed.
Of love and war discoursing, hap and need:

Yet from their thunder-tide the sated spright
Still to thy tempered woodlands takes its way
And turns for solace to thy leisured lay.

KEATS

If, in our English muster-roll of song,
Our nightingale was Shakspeare, Nature's son,
Milton our thrush, second (save him) to none,
Shelley our skylark lilting loud and long,
Thou wast the ousel of our tuneful throng,
That, in the solemn setting of the sun,
When all was silent else for day fordone,
Wakedst the woods with music sweet and strong.
Yet but brief time with us thou might'st abide:
Alack! La Belle Dame sans merci,
The wood nymph wild and sweet, the April-eyed
Strong sorceress, that men call Poesy,
Unsparing whom she loves ', had thee in thrall
And to her heaven too soon did thee recall.

SCHOPENHAUER

Thou, that hast weighed the world and found it nil,
That with the sword of thought hast rent apart
The inmost veil from off its quivering heart,
Meting the measure of its good and ill,
And as the leach that seeks to cure or kill,
Hast, to their eyes who shrink not from the smart
Of Truth's untempered, life-offending dart,
Bared all the workings of the wheels of Will;
The butt of brainless witlings who outright
All that's unflattering to their wit uncouth
And gross dull sense reject,—the mere dismay
Of those who fear to see the face of light,
Still in their hearts thou dwellest, come what may,
Who look for leading to the torch of Truth.

PARS POETAE

I.

I never could conceive why men should hold

The poet bound to don the huckster's dress
And tug and jostle in the motley press
Of the uncooked, to let himself be sold,
For gazing-stock, to idlers young and old,
Or with the mammon of unrighteousness
To truck and chaffer for a cheap success,
Which, gotten thus, were nought but flittergold.
An if the approof, to his endeavour due,
Be, as of right, vouchsafed by those (too few)
For judgment apt, 'tis well. But, if spite still
The voices of his peers, then those the wight
Must wait who shall come after and who will,
As without favour, judge without despite l.

II.

Nor with religions hath the poet aught
To meddle, whose religion is to do
Justly and to love mercy and the True,
Righteous and Fair still served to have and sought,
As his observance is, in word and thought
And action, from the world, as morning-dew.
Himself to hold unspotted nor ensue
The ways of men, where all is sold and bought.
The profane vulgar neither love nor hate
Shall he nor hearken to the scoffers' prate
Nor mingle with the vain uncaring crowd,
But with high thoughts his hungering soul shall feed
And Nature's voices list by mount and mead,
Thicket and waste, where lark and thrush are loud.

LOVE AND SONG

Needs must the poet early sing and late
Of Love, that is Life's spring and fountain-head,
Of Love, that dieth not, when all is dead,
That wreathes with flowers the sullen steps of Fate;
Nor, though the Fair he love and imprecate
Confusion on the Foul, upon his head
That evil doth no curse of him is said;
No room there is within his heart for hate.
Nay, since the most part of the poet's wit
From Love, that moves the stars, he hath to boon,
Still in the fair God's track his feet must run;
For song, that hath nor love nor faith in it,

To nothing may be likened but a moon
That unenlightened is of any sun.

SURSUM CORDA

I. SHAKSPEARE

In this our paltry day of dull pretence,
When no mere wage for noble work well done
Save by the Fates' sheer favour may be won
And he who serves the highest those, when hence
He's gone, who without favour or offence
Shall come and judge, must wait and else for none
To do him justice look beneath the sun,—
'Tis Shakspeare's self must give us confidence,
In that grim drama of the soul's despair,
Where Timon damns the inhuman human crew,
The Sursum Corda, from this modern hell
Our hearts that lifts into the upper air,
Who speaks,—"There is no time so miserable
"But that a man may yet in it be true."

II. RABELAIS

Up hearts! Refit and sail again the seas!
The soft mysterious pipe of birds at dawn,
The opening of the crocus on the 'lawn,
The April wind among the blossomed trees,
The cowslips gathering on the grass-grown leas,
These all, no less than Winter's woes bygone,
Witness to us how Life from Death is drawn
And how continuance Nature seeks, not ease.
He most in tune with her is, who, when wrecked
His hopes are, wastes no time in vain lament,
But of the wreckage builds the raft Content,
Wherewith to ride out the surge perilous
Of Life, and Pantagruel-like, confect
Is in contempt of things fortuitous.

HAFIZ AND PAUL

Two m my thought still linked together be,

Hafiz, the singer of the clustering vine,
And Paul, the mystic of the Gnostic shrine,
As being, both alike, in ecstasy,
Beyond the bounds of earth and sky and sea,
In contemplation of the things divine
Still rapt and drunken with the spirit's wine,
Calénders of the soul's debauchery.
And in this heaven I joy of old and new,
Where bard and prophet mingle good and ill,
Where Antioch Fars, where Hafiz joins with Paul
As being both deceivers and set true,
Both sorrowful and yet rejoicing still,
Both having nothing, yet possessing all.

WORDSWORTH

I.

In our loud times thy voice is little heard,
Singer of homely things and humbleness;
The roar of trade and strife, the battle's press
Well nigh thy memory from men's thoughts have blurred.
Yet, in life's pauses, like the mellow bird,
That, when the storm hath spent its wailing stress,
Sings in the setting from the wood-recess,
There cometh to our ears thy quiet word;
Thy quiet song, that tells of quiet days
And peaceful nights, with Heaven and Nature spent,
Far from Life's battle and the weary ways,
Where men for sorrow strive and miscontent,
And to our prisoned thought the worlds unbars,
That lie beyond the ether and the stars.

II.

Thy song is like the light of stars and moon,
Austere and pale and cold, belike, that show
To the hot blood: to others we must go
For the sheer splendours of the summer-noon,
The joys of May, the mellow nights of June,
When heaven above consenting, earth below,
With wine of rapture drunken, to and fro
Sway to the nightingale's ecstatic tune.
Too soft thou speak'st for youth's imperious ear;

It craves another and a stormier song:
But, when the leaves of life are falling sere,
The shriller songsters strike a note of wrong
For the tired sense, and to thy strain austere
It turns for still content and quiet cheer.

III.

Thou lov'dst the lowly of this world of ours;
The grazing herds, the flocks of sheep or geese,
The sunlight falling on some snowy fleece,
Thou sang'st, the wilder ways, the homelier flowers:
In Nature's less intoxicating hours
Most at thine ease thou wast; the slow increase
Of morning in the East, the quiet cease
Of daylight in the West, the evening showers,
More than the stormful sunset's thunderous towers
Or the sheer splendours of the Summer day
Gladdened thy soul: more than the frontispiece
The book thou lov'dst and from the heavenly powers
Sought'st, for the solace of thy pilgrim way,
The things that make for rapture less than peace.

IV.

Thou wast not glad; yet sorry wast thou not;
The note of all thy being plain content,
Peace without passion, as without lament,
The golden mean was betwixt cold and hot.
Enough for thee it was to know Life's what;
Its How thou soughtest not nor its intent,
But mad'st, amidst the days that came and went.
Thy heaven in common things ami common lot.
For us, whose lips have drained Life's cup of brine.
Thine aim too humble is, thy speed) too cold;
Yet, when the thought is purged by life's decline
And good and ill show clear, as we grow old,
We count thy water more than others' wine,
Thy silver more of price than others' gold.

V.

Others have struck a stronger note than thou,
With more ecstatic strains to hopes more high

Our hearts have raised and to the topmost sky
Have drawn our souls up from the worldly slough,
With Pythian songs of Nature's Why and How;
But thou alone hast taught us from things nigh
And common help to seek and to rely,
Not on what may be Then, but what is Now.
So, when all other voices have their soul
Of charm and healing lost, to thee we turn
And from thy word in peace contentment learn
To find and faith in Life's Eternal Whole
And Duty, Past and Present and To-be
Binding in chains of heavenly harmony.

HERMAN MELVILLE

None of the sea that fables but must yield
To Melville; whether with Whitejacket fain
We are to share, or Redburn, joy and pain;
Whether through Mardi's palaces, palm-ceiled,
We stray or wander in Omoo afield
Or dream with Ishmael cradled at the main,
High in the crow's-nest o'er the rocking plain,
Few such enchantments o'er the soul can wield.
But, over all the tale of Typee vale,
O'er all his idylls of the life afloat,
"The Whale" I prize, wherein, of all that wrote
Of Ocean, none e'er voiced for us as he
The cachalot's mad rush, the splintered boat,
The terrors and the splendours of the sea.

STÉPHANE MALLARMÉ

Friend of my youth, with whom I shared the chance
Of life for thirty years in joy and woe,
That hand in hand and heart in heart didst go
With me, though England's I and thou of France,
Thou hast fared on before me, in advance,
Into the mystic seas, to ebb and flow
Of time that answer not nor to and fro
Are shaken of the surge of circumstance.
Brother, farewell! I shall not see thee more;
I know that nevermore, for joy or pain
Our eyes shall meet, our hands shall clasp again;
Yet closelier, I doubt not, than of yore

Our souls shall join in some translunar sphere,
Where never Winter comes nor leaves are sere.

AIGUSTE VILLIERS DE L'ISLE ADAM

Villiers, old friend, strange spirit, weird but true,
Seeker of that which no man, new or old,
Of woman born might ever yet behold,
What sad sardonic Fate, in days undue,
Was it thy footsteps to the tomb that drew?
What Parcae, lustres nine scarce overtold,
Put thy fair lamp out, froze thy hot blood cold,
Whilst yet the light of life in thee was new?
Alack, the abyss, by Fate's relentless law,
Once gazed upon, the life to it doth draw.
And thou, beyond the bounds ol nights and days
Seeking, with Straining hands and eyes that yearn,
Hadst trespassed on the undiscovered ways
And looked upon the Land of No Return.

THEODORE DE BANVILLE

A songbird thou, if ever was there one!
Pure 'midst corruption, fearless 'midst affray,
Thou faredst still on thine unfaltering way,
In that sad France of thine, the self-undone,
Damned over self with victory never won.
A lark that never doubted of the day,
Thou sangest still, undaunted, on the spray
And through hate's mists look'dst ever for Love's sun.
Thou gav'st me love and comfort in the days
When my heart fainted for my soul's amaze;
Before mine eyes, bedimmed with sorrow's spell,
Thy hand it was that held hope's shining sign;
Nor ever shall I know thy parallel
For songful cheer and kindliness divine.

E. J. W. GIBB

Comrade, fare well, whose feet the untravelled East
Long time in equal measure trod with me!
From that fair land of flowers, where strand and sea

Shine with the sun of fable, last not least
Of those who for us Westerns spread the feast
Of Orient lore and Eastern poesy,
I ne'er shall look upon the like of thee
For love of song and care of bird and beast.
The pen is fallen from thine eager hand,
Death's finger laid upon the page undone:
Yet, in some interstellar Morning-land,
I doubt not but thy gentle soul shall find
Its earthly dreams fulfilled in heavenly kind,
Where Life and Death, where Love and Truth are one.

LECONTE DE LISLE

"Hope infinite," saidst thou, "doth Death contain".
When to Life's buttress-wall at the world's end
With death thou wonnest, Master mine and friend,
Whereas, Time's travel done, the soul full fain
Unto the eternal rest returns again,
What visions met thy view, what shapes did wend
Before thy glances, where the grey beach-bend
Of Life slopes down into Death's surgeless main?
Master, thou never shalt return to show
That which thou foundest in that shoreless sea;
Thou mayst not come to us; but we, to thee
O'erpassing, haply yet shall win to know
If there thy hopes accomplished thou didst see
Or the black night of blank Nonentity.

TRINITAS ANGLICA

Three names o'er all do glorify our land;
First his, whilere in England's mightiest day
Our stage illustrious over all for aye
Who made to many an undiscovered strand:
Next his, love, tears and laughter hand in hand
Unpeered to lead: and last, not least, to say,
His, on the canvas who in bright array
Set the whole glorious scheme by Nature planned.
Hereafterward, if any question make
Of thee what mm have,—most of all the men
Writ down for great upon the roll oi fame,—
For England's glory wrought with brush and pen,
These three tor thine exemplars shall thou take

And Shakspeare, Dickens, Turner shall thou name.

WITH A COPY OF SULLY PRUDHOMME'S "LES VAINES TENDRESSES"

Here, for such as will, are roses;
None of that bright host that flowers,
At the beck of sun and showers,
When the middle May uncloses
All the rapture that reposes
In earth's frost-enchanted bowers;
Such as in the shortening hours
Blow are these for Autumn's posies.
Yet, for some they have their featness,
Gentle souls that from life's madness,
From its cruel cold completeness,
From its hot hysteric gladness
Shrink, content from love and sadness
Still to crush a curious sweetness.

POPULARITY

To him, who seeks what is not bought or sold,
Who will not bow the neck in servitude
Nor pander to the unthinking multitude,
Approof comes seldom till his bones are cold,
Or, at the least, until he waxeth old,
Till hope is dead and may not be renewed
And all that life can show of fair and good
Dead leaves and ashes grown, like elfin gold.
So to the poet popularity,
Denied in youth and given when on the wane
Are life and hope, is like the promised fee,
So long withheld and paid at last in vain,
That damned Mehmoud to all eternity,
The gifts that crossed Firdausi's funeral train.

V.

UT PICTURA ....

PAN IM GEBÜSCH

(A PICTURE BY HANS THOMA)

What pip'st thou in the twilit thicket, Pan?
What dost thou here in this our day of June,
Thou that, long shut from sight of sun and moon,
Deforcing death's immitigable ban,
Revisitest the haunts and hours of man
And in our woodlands, where the ringdoves croon
Songs sad as life, re-trillst the olden tune
The blue bird fluted when the world began?
Back to thy grave, gray ghost, in Paxos Isle!
There, mid the moan of the Ionian main,
Under the sapphires of the Grecian sky,
All lapt and rounded with the warm sun's smile,
There dream thy dreams of sunny days gone by,
far from our sad wan world of strife and pain.

LE CAPUCHON ROUGE

(A PICTURE BY GREUZE)

When all the world was young and fair,
When all earth's rills ran honey-dew
And all the firmament was blue,
In Eden we together were.
Two lovers on youth's golden stair,
Love's only sweets, indeed, we knew
And nothing of his bitter brew,
Nor ever heard the name of care.
Yet fair and young art thou to-day:
Upon me from the canvas thee
With thy red lips and artless an.
Thou look'st as if the world should n'er
Grow old nor youth should pass away
And I, alack! my head is gray.

MEDEA

(A PICTURE BY F. SANDYS)

Vengeance, ye Gods! For I am wild with wrong-
Zeus, Here, Ares, ye celestial mates,
And Phoebus, thou, that in the morning's gates
Thronest, invincible of shafts and song,

And Cypris. that, as thou art sweet, art strong,
And ye, ye grim inexorable Fates,
That over Gods and mortals hold your states,
Help me, that have endured too long, too long!
Me of mine enemies but justify,
That have no reverence for the most high Gods,
No thought of justice or the Furies' rods:
Then, ye Immortals, with your fiery cars,
Come, snatch your maiden back unto the stars,
To dwell with you forever in the sky!

BACCHANAL

(A PICTURE BY ARNOLD BÖCKLIN)

Who loveth girls and golden song,
Here let him come and have his will!
The sun above the heavenward hill
Yet hangs, and all the meads along,
The Winegod leads his winsome throng.
The merry month is with us still;
The world without a doubt of ill
Is glad or thought of Winter's wrong.
Alack! What hath our grayness here
With this glad Paynimrie to pass,
Our Winter with its golden year,
Who of Silenus but his ass,
Who know of Momus but his rod,
His tigers of the tipsy God?

DER TOD ALS FREUND

(A PICTURE BY ALFRED RETHEL)

Near is the night of thy long day at hand.
Past is the Past, with all its joy and dole;
Life's mists are lifting from the appointed goal.
The sunset sleeps upon the slumbering land,
A mellow glory fall'n on sea and strand;
And with his hand of bone, Friend Death doth toll
The bell that parleys with the parting soul:
Almost the hour-glass empty is of sand.
Peace over all the landscape lies without
And peace within upon thy quiet end,

Life and its cares forgotten, hope and doubt,
Its storms all fallen stirless.—Heaven send
That, when my sands of life are running out,
Death by my side, as thine, may stand as friend!

GÖTTER IM WALDE

(A PICTURE BY MORITZ SCHWIND)

I cannot heal me of the haunting care,
The backward yearning for a bygone day,
When things yet lived which live no longer may,
When the young world was, in a younger air,
On Other wise than this our old world, fair,
Belike, 'tis idle; yet, in this our gray
Of modern lightlessness, mine eyes away
I cannot turn from the delights that were.
What boots the exile that 'twere wise to tell
Far from his fatherland content to dwell
Or him, that still in pine must live and die
In this our darklling dulness, he were well
Forget the Gods with whom, in dreams gone by,
He lived and loved beneath a brighter sky?

THE TWO POLES

Two poles of Art there be, the false, the true:
One negative, to whose plenipotence
Brute longing turns and sensual appetence
And humour shifting still from old to new:
The other, positive, the soul unto
Speaks and with Beauty sheer to heavens far hence
Above earth's mire uplifts the ennobled sense:
And all things gravitate between these two.
By this assay all spirits thou mayst test.
The high-tuned soul, in this our world of Will,
But Beauty follows, selfless and divine;
Whilst that to seek, which doth but interest
The Self, but stirs the ignoble sense, is still
The stamp and hall-mark of the Philistine.

INNOMINATA

(A PICTURE BY MARIANO FORTUNY Y MADRAZO)

A face upfloating through a shimmering sea
Of dreams, resurgent whether from the Past
Of Time, meknoweth not, or if forecast
Upon the Present's glass, as yet to be,
From the dim dreamland of Futurity.
But this I know, of women, first and last,
This only she from the Eternal Vast
Of the World's Soul it is that speaks to me.
These are her lips, whom I have sought in vain
Through many a devious waste of nights and days;
These are her starry eyes, whose wax and wane
Still were my beacons in the dreamland's ways;
And never shall I take her by the hand,
Until Death bring me to the Unknown Land.

THE RAPE OF PSYCHE

(A PICTURE BY PRUDHON)

What is yon slumbering maiden, wonder-white,
That, like a gossamer, through heaven fares,
Upborne and wafted of the frolic airs?
Psyche it is they bring, in brief delight
To dwell with Eros in his land of light.
Alack, poor maid, how many weary stairs
Must thou o'erclimb of toils and doubts and cares,
Ere full thy sense shall steep in thy lord's sight!
Sweet soul of the world's joys and woes, the hand
Of vengeful heaven is heavy upon thee.
True, Love is strong; but Fate supreme command
Hath over him nor suffereth him free
His own, or e'er, in darkness and in cold,
The appointed tale of sufferance be told.

JESUS ON LAKE GENNESARET

(A PICTURE BY EUGÈNE DELACROIX)

"Master, we perish!" was the cry. "Awake!"
And he, the mystic, heaven-deputed guest,
That slumbered, cradled on the billows' breast.

And dreamed, untroubled of the Storm-tossed lake,
Amid the winds' wail and the wild wave-break,
Of realms of peace beyond the golden West,
"Where is your faith?" said and the word, from rest
Rising, that stilled the raging waters spake.
Alack for unbelieving humankind!
How many a Hercules, without thru (are,
Hath wrought and perished, on the mountain side
How many a high Prometheus erst hath pined,
How many a Christ, exclaiming in despair,
"Where is your faith?" upon Life's cross hath died!

EDWARD BURNE JONES

"Nought is there better in this world than sleep,"
The Arabs say; "excepting death it be".
Sweet sleep in death and happy dreams to thee,
Fair soul, that still on earth didst vigil keep,
Life all too short the lovely shapes to reap,
That through thy brain went trooping ceaselessly,
Pleading in colour and in form to be
Bodied and rescued from the dreamland's deep!
The lovesome memories of a brighter day
Thou limnedst, to thy pencil, as my pen,
Dear, when more colour was in life and men
Were simpler than beneath our skies of gray.
Friend, may we meet in some serener land,
Where our lost dreams shall take us by the hand!

VALEDICTORY

(J. T. N., OB. AUG. 31, 1902)

Your name, set down among the names unknown
New-numbered of the innumerable rout,
Wherewith Death rounds our little lives about,
Falls on my heart, like the sepulchral stone.
You loved me not; nay, for your thought alone
You loved, your wayward thought, that would not out,
That mured you lifelong in a mist of doubt
And died with you, to blossom yet unblown.
Yet I, I loved you, as I loved my youth,
And with your death, though many a wave of days
And nights hath welled between our lives, since last

They met, yet somewhat of my Spring of sooth
And dream, methinks, into the darkling haze
Hath sunken of the insatiable Past.

VI.

VARIA

OUR DEAD

I.

Of those we've loved and lost too well we know
That they are gone to come again ho more,
That, in no future sky, no foreign shore,
The lapsing years to us again shall show
Their dear-beloved shapes of long ago:
We know that none of those who're gone before
Came ever back at Death's relentless door;
And yet we cannot let our darlings go.
Nor do we think that all in them we knew,
Which made them dear, by which themselves they weir.
Eyes, lips, hands, voice, breath, bosom, forehead, hair,
Not only back to earth, fire, water, air,
But, wrought in Nature's crucible anew,
Are gone to make earth green and heaven blue.

II.

If we could follow them where they are gone,
How should our lips their lips press in the rose?
How should oui- arms upon the wind wafts close,
Our eyes with theirs in green oi wood and lawn,
Our hands commingle in the flush of dawn?
When we, as they, of life, its joys and wot
Are free, far scattered to each breath that blows,
No longer held of flesh and blood in pawn,
Loosed from the let of hope, joy, doubt and pain,
Each atom of us free to fare and blend
With winds and watets, flowers and sun and rain,
Then may we look to be with them
And nothing will it profit us till then
But to endure with path the end.

WORK

Oft have I marvelled, in my sadder mood,
At reading, in the Scriptures of the Jew,

—The race that never yet set hand to do
That which of others done procure they could,
Drawers of water hewers nor of wood,
—Work worst set down of all that makes us rue,
For primal curse that men is born unto
Branded, for chiefest ill life's chiefest good.
Yet that the dictum of the Therapeut,
Of Paul, the Essenian doctor and adépt,
Whose speech for Christ, professing, we accept,
In these our days of vain hysteric heat,
I marvel more, hath borne such scanty fruit,
"Who will not labour, neither let him eat!"

IN MEMORIAM "ROVER", ob. JULY 2, 1902

My little gentle cat, whose eyes no dove
Might ever match for truth and tenderness,
Whose life was one long effort to express,
In thy mute speech, an overflowing love,
The wavering love of women far above,
I cannot think that death thy gentilesse
Hath ended all or that thy fond excess
In this thy ten years' span found scope enough.
I cannot credit that no soul in bond,
No thought there was behind those wistful eyes,
That pleaded for thy dumbness, as one cries
Out from Life's dusk into the dark beyond,
Nor doubt somewhen beyond the stars to find
The soul that lay those looks of thine behind.

MARTYRS OF HISTORY

I. HANNIBAL

Who on the page of history past doth pore
There much for sorrow findeth which doth call;
The world-Christ, drinking of the cup of gall,
Stretched through the ages on the cross of war,

Whilst plague, death, flood and famine, vultures four,
On his sad vitals prey: but, over all,
For what the hostile Fates with Hannibal
Wrought in the days bygone, my heart is sore;
Far Afric's godlike son, half Italy,
Though foiled of succour by his foes at home,
Twelve years who held against the might of Rome,
And then, recalled and baffled oversea,
Draining, for Carthage sake, the envenomed bowl,
To the high Gods gave back his glorious soul.

II. CÆSAR

Nor less for him I grieve of later years
That mightiest Julius, Rome's most goodly son.
Of all Life's nurslings sure the noblest one
That ever trod her stage of blood and tears.
That Caesar who, by witness of his peers,
E'er of free will endured to injure none,
Who, in all lands which be beneath the sun,
Came, saw and conquered hearts and eyes and ears.
And at the last, by envious I reverse,
Unto the foul assassin's bloody knife
Condemned to render up his noble In
Nor imprecation uttered neither curse,
But with his mantle veiled his mighty head
And "Et In, Brute!" sighed and so was dead.

III. COLUMBUS

He put off empire, like a worn-out wede,
For hero's wearing waxen overmean,
And as the Gods immortal and serene,
That breathe an air above man's lust and greed
Nor of the imperial purple stand in need,
To show as Gods upon the worldly scene,
With the bare grandeur of his soul beseen,
Sun-crowned abode in his accomplished deed.
When such as he their fetters wear for flowers
And for chief honour hold the scorn of men,
How should we lesser mortals, now as then,
Here, in this meaner martyrdom of ours,
But for sharp laurels Life's affronts espouse,
The thorn-set crowns that bind the thinker's brows?

IV. SAUL

Thy face we see but through the mists of hate
Save by the chronicles of jealousy,
Rancour and malice, nought we know of thee:
Yet may the eye of thought discriminate,—
Athwart the web, of lies and sorry Fate
Woven, wherefrom thy strong simplicity
In this waste world might never struggle free,—
One simply great as few on earth are great.
Nay, and methinks, thy mighty weary spright,
Clogged in the mesh of priestcraft and of guile,
So long on earth, when thou on Gilboa's height
With the sharp steel lett'st out, I see a smile
On thy stern face, as of a hero's soul,
Of Life content to be at last made whole.

V. PROMETHEUS

Primordial Saviour, Prometheus, thou,
That in the twilight of the morrowing earth,
Compassionate of mortal dole and dearth,
From thine immortal harbourage didst bow
And to the waste world's service, then as now
By the fierce Fates drained dry of joy and mirth
And peace and all that makes life living-worth,
Thyself by the fire's token didst avow;
Thee still on Caucasus the vultures tear
And still, eternal in the Eternal Aye,
Type of world's wont with all that's good and fair,
Skyward thy smile thou smil'st of sad disdain,
As the Gods knowing puppets of a day
And thee the true God on thy throne of pain.

VI. ROBERT EDMUND LEE

My thought, at this sweet season of the prime,
When hope and life new blossom, bark to thee,
My eager boyhood's hero, goeth, Lee.
Near forty years, since that thy strife sublime
Was sped, have passed and men well nigh thy time

And thee forgotten have. Yet take from me
This trilling tribute to thy memory,
This word of love and of memorial rhyme.
Alack, the wrong yet lives; the right is dead:
And nothing it availeth 'gainst the flood
Of Fate to fare: but this I know full well;
When in the last red field the free South fell
And liberty with her, the tears I shed
Come from mine inmost heart, not tears, but blood.

WO GÖTTER SIND NIGHT ....

"Whereas no Gods are, phantasms hold sway".
Thus he who sang of how the Eates did fill
To Wallenstein the cup of good and ill:
And so say I, in this our meaner day,
When all men worshipped once is passed away
Into oblivion and the idol Will
On our Olympus sole abideth still,
The one base God to whom we bend and pray.
Here, where, in darkness indisseverable,
Love, honour, faith are sunken and no light
Is left to guide us 'midst the utter gloom,
Save that of levins hurtling through the night,
The ways of phantasms of coming doom
Are full; our lives the larvae haunt of hell.

MENS ANGLICA

"You English have the passion of fair play",
Quoth France's daintiest living novelist.
How oft hath England what with armoured fist
From the embattled world she rent away
For conscience' sake back given again and aye
Bare thanks for magnanimity hath missed,
Foul thanklessness and hate, that might not list
But wax with benefits, but had to pay!
Yet she forbeareth; for forbearance still
The token is of the superior race
And magnanimity the mark of grace.
Like the Third Henry of the Valois line,
Betrayed she may be, often is, in fine,
But deceived never, rendering good for ill.

TO MAX EBERSTADT IN WILLESDEN CEMETERY

My thought to that sad January day
Goes back of half a score of years ago,
When underneath the newly melted snow
The last of that bright wit was laid away,
That eager thought, that with its sunny play
Of love and humour held our hearts aglow,
And we the last sad homage, here below
That loved thee, standing by thy grave, must pay.
Max, shall I never talk with thee again
Of all we loved and none enough but we,
Of Dickens, Dumas, Gautier, (peerless three!)
Liszt, Wagner, Schopenhauer? Woe is me!
How many a part of this sad heart and brain
Of mine is buried in thy grave with thee!

OX THE LIMPOPO. 1900

"We, that are Englishmen", he cried, "shall we
"Run from these dirty Dutchland dogs?" Scarce might
The little band that battled for the right
Against the ambushed foemen, one to three,
Make head, and some began to yield and flee;
When, with these words, into the middle fight
Rushed valiant little Plumer and the flight
Retrieving, of defeat made victory.
Three years have past since this brave deed befell;
Yet, trumpet-like, my heart the tale doth stir
With the assurance that, though heaven and hell
Combine against her, all with England well
Shall be, whilst yet such sons to succour her
She hath as Plumer, Powell, Kitchener.

TRANS ASTRA

Beyond the stars! What is beyond the stars?
We question still,—beyond those lamps of gold,
That all things mortal, whether new or old,
Shakspeare as Hafiz, England even as Fars,
Ruin as happiness and peace as wars,
With the like loveless constancy behold,

Each as the other pensive, pale and cold,
Venus as Mercury and Jove as Mars?
No more, grown sadly wise for clearer sight,
We look to find new heavens beyond the blue,
New Paradisal worlds of love and light;
Ourselves resign yet cannot plain on plain
But past the stars to seek of Space inane,
Through Time and Silence stretching still anew.

HERCULIS COLUMNÆ

Beyond Gibraltar strait, the narrow seas
'Twixt Spain and Africa, on either hand,
Guarding as 'twere, two mounds heaven-pointing stand
Of stone o'erweathered of the briny breeze,
The Pillars erst so-called of Hercules.
Hither the hero won and having scanned
Waters and skies nor sign of farther strand
Perceiving, for world's end erected these.
We of the Viking breed, for bound nowise
Content illimitable seas and skies,
As Hercules, to take, the world have gone
About, from set of sun to break of dawn,
And for new worlds to conquer still a-strive,
Are like to die of wistfulness, like Clive.

NEPIAEIMMA EONIKON

How long shall we the pregnant words o'erhear,
Unheeding, in the Hebrew Writ that stand,
"The poor shall never cease out of the land"?
How long silk purse to fashion of sow's ear
Strive and to cause the dregs of race run clear?
How long with dulcet speech and usance bland
Seek to tame rat and wolf, that understand
No law but force, that know no faith but fear?
When shall we learn that kindness cruelty
Sheer is to him that is his passions' slave,
That from himself there's nothing him can save,
From Death's red furnace-mouth and ruin's maw,
But discipline, enforcing Truth's decree,
And stern fulfilment of an equal law?

LOVE AND REASON

"A woman, at some time of year, 'tis true,
"Is necessary; but no business make
"Of her." Thus Fletcher's stout old soldier spake,
In those plain times when all of what all do
Were not ashamed to speak, nor that, from view
B) hiding, thought to quell, for prudery's sake,
Which from the very source its root doth take
Of natural life in all things old and new.
Could we but live by sage Leontius' saw
And in our loves unto attemperan e hold
And reason keep and understanding's law,
What states had thriven, that fell to ruin red,
What hearts were warm, that long ago are cold,
What faiths and hope were live, that now are dead.

"SPORT"

"But for amusements, life were tolerable",
So said the sage; and certes, what in court
And hall and street "amusement" men report
Is weariness for those, past words to tell,
To whom true pleasure is delectable
And highest, noble work; whilst, what for "sport"
Alas! is holden of the baser sort,
What for the nobler sense were direr hell
Than our dumb fellows' pain to see, to hear
The rabbit's scream, the hare's despairing cry,
To meet the dying bird's fast-glazing eye,
Reproachful for its life of harmless cheer
Crushed out by fools, who nothing better know
Than to find pleasure in another's woe?

SPES CRUDELIOR

Except for hope, our lives at peace might be.
Worst gift of the sardonic Gods to men,
That of the Nine Beatitudes mak'st ten,
For that of all creation blest is he
Who nought expects, we should not, but for thee,
NOW possible neglect for hopeless THEN;
We should not wallow in the worldly fen,

When with desire despair off-cast might we.
Excepting thou into the fruitless fight
Urgedst us back, we long aside had laid
The hopeless stress toward the mocking light,
That still, the more we follow, more doth fade.
And an eternal harbour for the spright
In Resignation's sanctuaries had made.

FALSE SLAVERY AND TRUE

Much in these prating times of ours hath been
Of slavery discoursed and sung and writ,
But mostly, as meseems, with little' wit.
For if (as surely), slavery service mean,
Who is there here but serveth? king and queen,
Peasant and noble, all in service knit
Each unto other, as is well and fit,
So but the wage do to the work convene.
One slaver)' but there is, of all that be,
Intolerable, making Gods to weep,
The slavery of the wise and passion-free
To those that serve their lusts, of good to ill,
Noble to base. From such a slavery still
God of His grace our kindly England keep!

CATKIND AND HUMANKIND

My rat, that sits am! sleeps upon my knee.
For sheer intelligence, with men I know
Not only can compare, but, high or low,
Few reach his standard of morality.
That which [do for him he renders me
With low and faith such as few humans show,
Rejoices when I come and when I go,
Cries at my door nor comforted will be.
His spreading ruff, his bushy tail and hair
For vanity sufficing him content:
He does not pine the power with me to share
Nor on the delegation is he bent,
—To harass me who pay for him and care—
Of representatives to Parliament.

THE CREATION OF WOMAN

When God an end of making man had wrought,
Flesh of His flesh and blood of His own blood,
He looked upon His work and deemed it good;
Then, overcasting in His pregnant thought
That which in time yet unaccomplished brought
To pass should be, how that His handwork should
Himself defy and in his upstart mood,
Vie with his maker, sighed and knew it naught:
Yet that His glorious work might not undo;
But, casting round for a device whereby
He might forefend Him from His creature new,
Bethought Him to his strivings to apply
A check and woman made, to clog his wings
And hinder him from over-venturings.

RIGHTS AND DUTIES

Long of their rights alone have we to men
Enough discoursed; yea, overlong about
To stir their souls to discontent and doubt
Have gone, till all our world is as a fen,
With exhalations foul and meteors' vain
Of wish and will fulfilled, a rabble-rout
Of sensual dreams wherein no grass will sprout,
No flowers will blow, fruit ripen neither grain.
Them of their duties, surely, to bespeak
High time it is, of duty,—moon and sun
Which holdeth in their course of day and night,
Which is the star of life for strong and weak,—
And that high prophet's speech, who said, "No right
"Is but ariseth from a duty done."

NATURA NATURANS

Nature concerns herself not much with man.
So but the stream of race run full and free,
All's well for her; the individual she
Leaves for himself to shift as best he can.
"Sleek men, that sleep o' nights", best fit her plan,
(As Caesar's), such as unconflictingly,
Bound to the car-wheels of the Will-to-Be,
Eat, drink and slumber out their little span.

Of this it is that she, from birth to death,
The human animal still pampereth,
—Those, in whom soul place over body claims,
Rebating,—and that women, who the tools
Immediate are, by which she shapes her aims,
Do for the most part love and tender fools.

ON THE SOUTH AFRICAN HORSE-HOLOCAUST

Of all these grim three years of grief and gore,
There's nought so stirs the source of tears in me
As the sad myriads from oversea
Of horses brought, to perish without store.
Ah, England of my love, my heart is sore
To think what load of penance laid on thee
In the grim Future, what calamity,
Dearth, famine, pestilence, intestine war,
Must for the wrongs of the true horse atone,
Man's patient, loving slave, for faith inbred
And native virtue worth a world ol Boers,
Forsaken on the arid Afric moors
Offcast to die, despairing and alone,
With the vile vultures hovering round his head.

HILLFOOT AND SUMMIT

If there's a good on earth, it is content.
'I never was content, i'faith, not I!
"No hillside was too steep, no peak too high,
"But I must buckle to for the ascent.
"So hath Fate fooled me to my topmost bent;
"For Life is like an Alp; one peak past by,
"Another towers higher 'gainst the sky,
"Between the climber still and his intent."
How better far to tarry in the vale
And from the base the mountain-top to view!
There, at the least, the sky's not gray, but blue;
The sun is warm and bright, not chill and pale,
As in the summit's over-subtle air;
And one is spared the swink of getting there.

PAST, PRESENT, FUTURE

Here have we but the Present: with the Past
Nor with the Future our concernments are.
Past is the Past, the Future overfar.
Since that which now is with us will not last,
Why leave unjoyed the life that flits so fast,
Why from the sight of sun and moon and star
Hide in the dark, when all before us are
The deserts of Eternity the vast?
Why with the Past concern us, since Time's plough,
Present and past, the selfsame soil doth ear
And the same fruits of joy and pain doth rear?
Why with the Future? Since foregoing men
Were no wise happier when the Now was Then,
How were we happier, if the Then were Now?

OIGNEZ VILAIN, IL VOUS POINDRA ....

"Caress a churl", the ancient adage says,
"And he will cuff you. Cuff him till he yell,
"And he'll caress you". If you've wit to spell
The meaning of these words, in Life's wild ways
Safe shall you walk and easance have and praise.
But, if you use not as the saw doth tell
And with the vulgar seek by doing well
And love to commerce, you will reap amaze;
Yea, for repentance cause you shall enough
Have and your life long feed on bitter food
Of hatred and contempt; for everywhen
Of one consent 'twas holden of wise men
That everywhere the base unthankful chuff
Ill offices returneth still for good.

JUNE 11, 1903

Servia, thou name-devoted, sorry LAND
Of Seres to their own lusts, how long with thee,
In the sad name of lawless Liberty,
Shall Gods and men endure? How long, unbanned,
Unblasted of His thunders, shalt thou stand,
In the sheer sight of heaven and earth and sea,
Outraging all that right and truth decree,
With ravin-reddened brows and bloody hand?
Since men forbear thee, since the avenging Same

Of heaven yet laggeth, I, that see and hear
Midmost my dream and shudder, in the name
Of all whose hearts with love and pity stir,
Ban such as thou, thou woman-murderer,
Back to that nether hell from which they came.

ENGLAND'S GOD

I.

Lord, Thou, indeed, hast been our dwelling-place,
From generation unto generation.
The confluence of nation upon nation,
The storm diluvian of race on race,
That, since our Britain, on her island-base
Throned, hath the world for her inhabitation
Taken, have striven to shock us from our station,
We had not, save with Thee, availed to face.
"What is this God?" The envious nations question.
"Sure none of those to whom we bend the knee
"'Tis that this little people to the gestion
"Of all the world hath brought from sea to sea,
"That hath their governance ordained to be
"Beyond opposing and above contestion?"

II.

Our God is none of yours: no Baal uncouth,
No Moloch, Allah, Jahveh, Adonaï,
Such as, his thunder-summits of Sinái
Forsaking in the world's unhistoried youth,
Taught men the love of hate, the scorn of ruth,
That burned and slew in Jericho and Aï;
No earless Norns we serve, no eyeless Graiai;
Our England's God is loyalty and truth.
These are our Elohim, alone perduring
O'er all Gods else, that are but for a day:
Leant on their help, disdaining passion's luring,
Built hath our Britain her imperial sway;
Nor, whilst she standeth fast on their assuring,
Her faith shall fail, her power shall pass away.

LIBERTY, EQUALITY, FRATERNITY

(THREE SONNETS ON THE REPUBLICAN FORMULA)

I. LIBERTY

No one of woman born was ever free;
The good to their own goodness and the ill
To their own lusts and passions slaves were still
And bondmen both to that which is to be.
Grim Anarch of our lives, Necessity,
Thou whose stern shade the halls of heaven doth fill,
That bendest all unto thine iron will,
To whom no Gods there are but bow the knee,
How shall a worm like man his little day
From thine enforcement study to withdraw?
None is there free, beneath thine iron law,
Save the sad sage, who, in the Lustral fires
Of lonely thought hath purged his lusts away,
The world discarded and forsworn desires.

II. EQUALITY

Equality! Another idle word,
A phrase, wherewith the unflinching egoist
Feeds fools and dupes the dullard at his list.
In any age, since first Creation stirred
With breath and life, when was it seen or heard
That two in heart were equal, wit or fist?
Set Shakspeare by the modern journalist,
Briton by Burgher, lark by (anion bird,
Aryan by negro? Was there ever drone
So dull, though equal all in talk hold he.
That shaped his practice by his theory,
Chief Aristocrat Nature but must own,
Who, with each act, each voice, her fierceliest
Equality a lie doth still protest?

III. FRATERNITY

Fraternity! Ah, that, at least, is true;
Nor yet alone of human brotherhood,
But of all things created, ill and good.
The mild dumb brutes, that serve us and to due
But for some dole of food and shelter sue;

The pismire in the sand, the insect-brood,
Birds in the bowery height and wolves in wood,
These all claim brotherhood with me and you.
Sweet sister-name of Love, which (Dante says)
Hath made and moveth stars and moon and sun,
Of Love, that lodestar of our darkling days,
Without whose lighting life for us were none,
Ah, might the watchword of the Future be
That keynote of the soul, Fraternity!

TWO WAYS OF LOVE

Most love is like a stormy Summer day,
That roars and blusters through the hours of light;
Then, when the slackening sun brings on the night,
Without word spoken, falls and dies away;
Nor is there aught of all its tyrant sway,
Save some few lopped-off boughs, that meets the sight,
And haply some stray bird, struck down in flight;
But all 'tis gone, as if it were not aye.
Yet Love, that's worth the name, is othergate:
Like an October day, more gently fair
And less unstable than the Summer's glare,
It till the night prolongs its sober state;
And when with evening needs it must abate,
Affection's sunset glorifies its air.

CONSCRIPT AND VOLUNTEER

Be mindful, England, of thy heroes dead,
Who on the sun-dried deserts oversea
Lie, slain of cunning or of treachery.
In all thine isle of mists and manlihead
Scarce was a household but one darling head,
Heedless of aught but truth and loyalty,
Gave unrepining up for love of thee,
Thy wounds to med'cine with its best blood shed.
Be mindful, over all, that these were none
Who by the iron rod of ruthless law
Were driven as sheep into the red blind maw
Of ravening war; nay, each, clerk, peasant, peer,
Of his free will left all that makes life dear,
To die for thee beneath the Afric sun.

"A MAD WORLD, MY MASTERS!"

This world a cage is (old Bandello says)
Full of an infinite variety
Of fools. Since God made heaven and earth and sea
And setting folly in the place of praise,
The world's brows with a fool's cap bound for bays,
Was ever such a rabble-rout to see
As that which squeaks and gibbers, fancy-free,
In these our Will intoxicated days?
Midas of old was fain his asses' ears
To hide nor bared his blame for all to know:
But now each coxcomb, when the maggot spurs,
In hall and highway, mail and Streel and school.
Goes glorying in his shame and crying, "Lo!
"With what a peerless grace I play the tool!"

LUX IN ANIMÂ

The sage, sole-sitting in the forest hoar,
Moveless and mute, beneath the banyan-tree,
The world forsworn and all its vanity,
Fixeth his thought upon the unknown shore
Whereto our lives, returning evermore,
Are merged again in the unbottomed sea,
The shoreless ocean of Eternity,
That round our little day doth plash and roar.
Still through the years he sitteth, stark and dumb,
Till there a light ariseth in his soul,
Which, waxing aye, as in a flaming scroll
Graven, discov'reth him Life's secret sum,
Concentred in this word ineffable,
"In thee alone are Gods and Heaven and Hell."

MY LADY DEAD

I.

Never any more to see your face;
Never any more to hear you speak;
Never any more to feel your cheek
Pressed against my cheek in our embrace;

Never any more the kissing-place,
Where your throat the softly-rounded peak
Of your chin joins, with my lips to seek;
Never any more to greet your grace;
Never any more, with love aglow,
Never any more your eyes to meet;
Never any more to see you go
Hither, thither, with your flitting feet;
Never any more to let you know
How I love you, o my sweet, my sweet!

II.

When they say to me that you are dead.
Bid me take of you a last good-bye,
Look my last upon you, as you lie,
Ere they nail the lid down on your head,
Nought I answer; not a tear I shed;
Nay, I smile to think of how they lie.
How should you, indeed, be dead and I
Standing here alive beside your bed?
Surely, truth will not bide falsehood aye;
Sure, what real is from what doth seem
Yet shall sundered be for us some day:
Yea, if God be righteous as I deem,
Surely, you will wake and smile and say,
"All was but a dream, a dreary dream!"

VEDANTASARA

I.

Unto his soul, that on the Alpine heights
Of the Vedanta hath his harbourage found
And by the Indian Wisdom hath unwound
The veils that be about the bight of bights.
The knowledge, which from hope of heaven's delights
And dread of hell's affearments doth redound
To free the imprisoned spirit, in this round
Of darksome da) confined and careful nights,
The world and all its creatures, jo) and v.
Its baseless hopes and fears, its ill and well,
Axe as a vain phantasmagoric bow.
That answers to the omnipresent spell
Of the One Self, midst all that come and go,

Alone unchanging and perdurarable.

II.

Yea, cognizant he is that, on this side
The evolution of the Self, Gods are
And heaven and hell and sun and moon and star
And what worlds else beyond the skies abide,
Which, at Its hest as erst they lived and died,
Evenso for ever It shall make and mar,
Æon by aeon still, in space o'er far
And time for thought to follow over wide.
Thus to the Selfless Soul all Gods must bow,
The One sole-throned where erst the many sat,
And in thought's cruset molten, old and new,
Religions all resolved be unto
The all-involving dictum, "That art Thou",
Whose golden obverse readeth, "Thou art That".

III.

Cold is the air upon those Alps of thought,
And he, for his soul's health who harboureth there,
Must, ere his lips can breathe that ether rare,
Cast off concern of all that here is wrought
And all that is of mortals prized and sought,
And putting by earth's tests of foul and fair,
Himself address unto the only care
The Truth to seek, than which all else is nought.
But here to find, for those who seek, is Light,
The eternal Light of conscious Selflessness,
Which, once enkindled in the enraptured spright,
From heart and brain the darkness doth expel
Of ignorance and doth the soul possess
With peace, indwelling, inenarrable.

IV.

What can be likened to his ecstasy,
Beside his bliss ineffable, as wind
What earthly joys are not, upon whose mind,
After long continence, the things to see
Behind the veil vouchsafed, 'tis borne that he
The Self Undifferenced is, with which he pined
To be made one. and nowhere else to find,

Save in himself, Gods, hell and heaven be.
Thenceforth, for him an end of doubt and strife
There is; thenceforth as life is death and life
As death; thenceforth, with the Eternal Whole
For evermore incorporate and one,
The Light Supernal shineth in his soul,
That is beyond the light of moon and sun.

THE END OF THE ÆON

The end of the old order draweth nigh;
The air is thick with of coming chan
Foreboding le through all men's fancies range,
Dim clouds of doubt, that overcast the sky,
And mists of fear, that darken ever) eye.
In hut and hall, in town and tower and gragne,
Men's souls an ick with visions void and strange,
Delirious dreams oi those about to die.
No faith there is but is a phantom grown
Of its old self: the Gods by doubt and Fate
Axe frozen back to shapes of senseless stone.
All eyes are fixed upon the Future's gate,
For that which is to be, and all things wait
To hail the coming of the Gods unknown.

THE RETURN OF THE GODS

Methinketh, yet, our time of toil and pain
Shall pass and all the clouds of care and spleen,
That, since the coming of the Nazarene,
Over the blighted earth have brooding lain,
Shall melt away and life grow glad again.
The sun shall have its primal Pagan sheen
And in a world new-ransomed and serene,
The old frank friendly Gods return to reign.
Back to Time's limbos heaven shall fare and hell;
Zeus shall smile down on us from sapphire skies
And joy have leave once more with men to dwell:
Phoebus shall cheer us with his cloudless sight
And Cytherea with her starry eyes,
And Eros have again his ancient right.

THE RETURN TO BARBARISM

In the world's youth, men rule by count of head;
The ignoble many crush the finer few
And all confusion is 'twixt false and true,
Till certain of the wise, the state nigh dead
Reviving, with much toil and much blood shed,
Law's checks impose upon the unruly crew,
And wholesome governance and order due
Grow with the rule of those to ruling bred.
But, in its second childhood, children like,
Authority and discipline that spurn
And in their appetites uncurbed will be,
The world descends again into the dyke
And wallows, swine-like, in the lewd return
To barbarism of democracy.

EDUCATION TRUE AND FALSE

The cry in this our dear quack-ridden day
For popular education is, and we,
Whose backs already overburthened be,
Must needs, to educate the castaway
In French and Greek and freehand drawing, pay,
And that each liege his leisures may at gree
Charm with cat-consternating harmony,
Banjo and mandoline must teach him play.
Meanwhile, some minor matters, which of yore
Not without weight and import holden were,
Omitted are from our arbitrament,
Nor to the commons teach we any more
Such toys as reverence for good and fair,
Truth, honour, manners, modesty, content.

THE DAY OF SMALL THINGS

Small is our age for better and for worse:
Small in its good, as in its wickedness;
Small in its aim, in its performance less:
Small is its benison and small its curse;
Its art is small and smaller yet its verse.
Small are its men and women, strife and stress,
And small its thoughts, hopes, fears, wish, carefulness;
Nought hath it great, save vanity and purse.

So, with its little sweets, its little strife,
In little goods and ills, its little spell
Shall it outfool: and when the term assigned
Accomplished is, of this its paper life,
Once flared away in Time's unpitying wind,
Leave but a little ash and an ill smell.

THE NEW INVASION OF THE BARBARIANS

When I consider this our modern whirl,
Where all the links of life are rent apart
And all things holy, honour, faith, love, art,
Cower at the mercy of the invading churl,
Meseems, the Huns once more I see unfurl
Their banners on the heights, ere to the heart
Of the old world they surge and town and mart
And temple swamp with their resistless swirl;
Save that, to day, no saving streams there come,
Fresh from Life's fountain-head, the world's repair
To work; but from the abysses of Time's sea
The rotting wrecks of race, the ages' scum,
Float up upon the flood and fill the air
With the miasmas of putrescency.

SUPERSTITION

Those who at superstition use to rail
Are blind and deaf to all that is of yore
Recorded of the unrelenting war
Waged by the ruthless Fates against the frail
Sad sons of man,—who, that they might not fail,
Must from sheer sufferance learn the spells that o'er
Their foes unseen prevail;—nor know, this lore
Obscure, they scoff at as an idle tale,
The sum, upon experience's page
Deep-charactered, of thought, in many an age,
Concentred on the endeavour is to find
The natural magic which propitiates
And of their dreadful purpose baulks the blind,
Deaf Gods, the eyeless and the earless Fates.

PROGRESS .... OVER THE CLIFF

Meseems,—in this our democratic day,
When every wholesome check against abuse,
All lawful reverence and kindly use,
From wiser times inherited, away
Are swept, to give men's lusts the freer play,
When open stands Will's Revolution-sluice
And every dunce full freedom to the deuce
(None other!) has of going his own way,—
The world is like to one that stands, blindfold,
On a cliff-edge, above a raging deep,
What while his fellows hearten him be bold
Nor back a step for sake of safety go,
But, in the name of Progress, o'er the steep
Push on and plunge into the abyss below.

TURK AND SLAV

Ne'er could I deem the Turk "unspeakable",
treason foul he did in blood repress.
Nor wherefore "Slav" should "angel" spell might guess
Here a folk have we, sober, honourable,
True, clean, brave, honest, all that's fair and well,
And there a race name-doomed, for drunkenness
Theft, sloth, tilth, treachery branded and do less
Stained with a soil of lust indelible.
Dark are the days and all the dim To-be
With murk of doubt o'ermisted is for me:
Natheless, I hope to see the conquering Turk,
Regenerate, yet the dregs of Slavdom bring
Back to the one sole necessary thing,
Duty in quiet done and wholesome work.

THE LAST OF THE GODS

Of all the Gods, for Love my heart is sore,
For Love, that was so frank and fair a thing,
That had so vague and sweet a voice to sing
To our tired sense. Since to the unknown shore,
With all his glamours, he is gone before,
How shall the world again be glad in Spring,
How shall the earth again with blossoming
Be clad or have delight of Summer more?
And yet, and yet, sad heart, be comforted:

Love, of a truth, is not for ever dead;
He sleepeth but for weariness of woe
And sheer despite of this our world of show
And yet will lift again his lovesome head
And take again his arrows and his bow.

THOUGHT AND TRUTH

Few for themselves there are who think and fewer
Who an abstract idea can receive
And follow, unconditioned, who can cleave,
For their life's guidance, unto duty pure
And natural truth, unqualified by lure
Of heaven or threat of hell, but, to believe,
Must clutch at some God's garments nor to leave
Their mythologic crutches can endure.
To harbour on the snow-clad heights of Truth,
Alone with the bare soul, and in the thought
To delve for knowledge of the Must and Ought,
This is the portion of the few, forsooth,
Who in those lands of light can breathe and bear
The coldness of that interstellar air.

PERSONALITY

Most of all things which threaten in Death's Must,
We dread the loss of personality.
Though, in our own despite, we know that we,
Once dead, like all things else, must rot and rust
And mingle with the everlasting dust,
That is the stuff of earth and heaven and sea,
Nor evermore return ourselves to be
What once we were, the just as the unjust;
Yet, to the thought of some vague power we cleave,
Beyond the clouds, at will that can unweave
The warp and weft of Nature and of Fate,
Nor can our selves abandon nor forswear
The meeting at the Morning's golden gate
With those who here of us belovéd were.

THE GOD OF THE PAST

A tyrant slave bound to the wheels of Fate,
Forever forced to be all creatures' bane,
The eternal spring of grief and woe and pain,
The minister of universal hate
And terror, still 'twixt man and man breedbate
And brute and brute to be, for ever fain
His own and all things' misery to ordain,
In His immortal self reduplicate
The Maker, at whose will the world He made
Was doomed in hell, for faults ol Him foresaid,
To burn, Himself self-doomed, in chains self-cast,
With all thing' curses heaped, a baleful life
To lead, with all as with Himself at strife;
Suck was the God whose power is of the Past.

THE GOD OF THE FUTURE

I.

Lord, though I may not look upon thy face,
Yet, in my dreams, against the Future's sky,
I see Thee throned aloft; and to the eye
Of faith and hope, defying time and space,
As in the East the unrisen sun we trace,
Thy figure fills the horizons far and nigh,
A God for those who live, not those who die,
A God of love and life and light and grace.
Thou, that shalt come, of hate and doubt and strife
To free the world and from the ages' ban
Of dole to unspell our sorrow-darkened life,
That shalt uncharm the sun and in thy train
Love to his primal empire bring again,
Hail, that shalt be whole God, because whole Man!

II.

In the old ages, men their spirit's goal
With temples builded to the zenith sought
And with their skyward fiower-spikes, graven and wrought
From fret of soulless granite into soul,
Still upward strove, as knowing not Thy whole
Sweet heaven spheral, as in life is nought
Of fair and good, but to the eye of thought
The eternal symbol shows from pole to pole:
But, with Thy coming, Thou shalt cause them know

Thy heaven around and in us, not above
Our foreheads only, but our feet below,
And to our thought wings giving as a dove,
The world and all therein to us shalt show
One lane illimitable of light and love.

VII.

THE SILVER AGE

I.

The memories of the Age of Gold,
The age of innocence and glee,
Of primal peace and purity,
Whereof whilom the poets told,
Wellnigh within our hearts are cold:
No more of its return dream we
Nor that Life ever young might be
Can we conceive, that now is old.
Yet, at threescore, a purer page
Of life we reach, a stiller shore,
Where Passion's storms no longer rage
And peace, at last, we have once more:
If not the Golden, at threescore
We have, at least, the Silver Age.

II.

To tell again the tale of things long told,
To tread in thought the over-travelled ways,
To shrink with shame to think in bygone days
How oft night's treasure in the dawn-light cold
To nought hath shrivelled, even as elfin gold,
Life's sombre fairy tale with sad amaze
To overread by hope's declining ra)
These are the occupations of the old.
Yet that there is in eld which doth console
For all that life must leave and lose with youth.
The end of hopeless hoping, the surcease
Of strife and stress, the clearer air of truth,
That floods the heart, the sunset in the soul.
That on life's passing sheds its light of peace.

III.

In my hot youth, no flowers beneath our skies
Of daily life and use would serve my turn,
No bluebells nodding in die golden fern,
No violets purple as my lady's eyes,
No roses ruddy as her lips: the prize
For which I longed by earthly mead or burn
Was not to seek, but in the fields etern
It flow'red, the asphodel of Paradise.
But, now that youth is past and age draws on
And the hot blood grows cool for Time's relent,
No more I sigh for blossoms in no land
That ever blew on which the sunlight shone,
But make my shift with that I have in hand,
The flow'rage of the plant of Sad Content.

IV.

Oft do men say, when age hath given them pause,
Lapsed life still willing Time to them restore,
"Had age youth's ableness, youth age's lore!"
Of all the idle Will-begotten saws
Surely the idlest! By the eternal laws,
Fools, were life given you to live once more,
That would you do which you have done before,
For that the effect ensueth still the cause.
Youth is to eld and unto youth is age
As Spring to Winter and to Winter Spring.
Wrote not the Winter pause upon the page,
The world were burned away with blossoming.
So after Life comes Death, its seeding-stage,
The darkling half of its unending ring.

V.

In my young days I loved the winter-cold:
The laggard mornings and the languid rays
Of the pale sun, well nigh too weak the haze
To pierce, were dearer to me than the bold
Upmounting dawns of June and the fierce gold
That overflooded all the August ways:
To me the long, still nights, the darkling days
A tale of dreamful peace and mystery told.
But now, youth gone, I languish for the sun,
Like my old hound, that loves at length to lie

And bask and feel the blessed fluid heat
Through all his age-chilled veins and arteries run,
Ere yet the harbingers of death drawn nigh
To the faint heart creep up from the cold feet.

OCULO RETORTO

If I might turn the river of the years
Back to its fountain-head and at the spring
Of the Prime Cause drink life's requickening,
I would not seek from the consenting spheres
Lost youth, with all its idle smiles and teal
Nor with dead Love prevail again to sing
His syren songs of sempiternal Spring,
Nor crave return of manhood's hope and fears.
I would but ask to draw yet once again
The full fresh breath of frank and fearless life,
to feel once more, now time is on the wane,
Unmarred by any sense doubt or strife,
The innocent, the ignorant disdain,
The child-unconsciousness of joy and pain.

ET EGO ....

Though long ago it is, God wot,
Since I at Cupid's altars knelt,
I, too in Arcady have dwelt
And shared whilere the lover's lot;
Nor, though the blood no more is hot
Within my veins, that I have smelt
Its roses and its breezes felt
Yet in my dreams have I forgot.
Nay, in this life of every day,
Anon, the old Elysian strain
Makes for a breathing-space its way
The mists of eld and usance through
And I in Arcady am fain
Awhile to live and love anew.

LUCUS DEORUM

I.

To those who live, as I have lived, alone,
With birds and music mated, books and flowers,
By their own heart-beats all the changing hours,
Rain and shine, measuring, strange things are shown;
Their ears to many an other-worldly tone
Resound, and touched by the supernal powers,
Their eyes o'erlook this shadow-world of ours
Into the spheres beyond, the ways unknown:
Their hopes possess another world than this
Dull orb of day and night; in wake and dream,
Their hands lay hold on the Invisible;
Thought wings with them the ultimate abyss,
That lies to thitherward the icy stream,
And opens Heaven to their gaze and Hell.

II.

Yet more of Heaven than Hell, to Love the praise!
Their dreams: though by the inexorable Fates,
Unfriended, lacking of their spirit's mates,
Foredoomed to fare this round of, nights and days,
The yearning in their souls, from dull dismays
Of common lusts removed and common hates,
Hath drawn Love down from utter Heaven's gates,
To walk with them the weary worldly ways.
So, in his hand, across Life's sorry stage
They pass, unspotted of the paltry age,
And by his guidance, for their spirits' food
Seeking the fair, the wise, the true, the good,
Dwell, with the souls of hero, prophet, sage,
In a Gods' grove of sacred solitude.

PORTO INVENTO

The time is sick with toil and care and sin;
Life's arteries are choked with doubt and strife;
In all its ways Will's brambles, thick and rife,
Hinder his feet that fain to peace would win;
The world without is rotten and within.
No drug will serve; the canker of our life
Calls for the mercy of the surgeon's knife;
The case is past the approof of medicine.
But we, our day to evening drawing near,
Time taught the real from the things that seem

To know, absolved from hope and doubt and fear,
Here in this backwater of thought we dream,
Content to suffer, with unsorrowing eye,
Life's senseless whirl of chances lapse us by.

HYPNEROTOMACHIA

Bytimes from this my dream I wake
And look on life, as it goes by,
Beneath the wondering, pitying sky,
And pity, too, on men I take;
Yea, fain, to ease my spirit's ache,
To venture out with them I sigh
And to the Gods lift hand, that I
May succour them for sorrow's sake.
Alack! In vain to heaven I sue:
What have they, this with that, to do,
The world, with all its troubled streams
Of strife and turmoil, old and new,
Its things that are, its things that seem,
And I, a dreamer with my dream?

LIFE'S SUMMING-UP

I.

"Life is too short for question", quoth the sage;
"Laugh and let be!" The saw is simple sooth:
And now, indeed, less worthy wrath than ruth,
All things set down upon the ended page,
I find its record; for the years assuage
The ardent indignation of hot youth.
To-day no more I blame the Fates uncouth
Nor heaven inhospitable accuse: I rail
No longer at the Gods, as knowing they,
For all their pride and pomp of high estate,
Are, even as we creatures of a day,
But bondmen of inexorable Fate,
And once their term accomplished, even as we,
Under the dust of doom must buried be.

II.

Nor do I rail at life and fellow-men:
No more the page accomplished I re-read,
The script of done and undone, stress and need,
Nor overthink the wrongs endured erewhen.
To all which is and was I say "Amen!"
What matters it? The Past is past indeed
And the ripe age's all-atoning reed
With manhood's Now hath overwrit youth's Then.
But this I know, that, life for me once done
And I, work ended, safe in the domain
Back of the Selfless Whole, ' no Will-to-be
Shall lure me forth to look upon the sun
Nor aught avail with me to wear again
The vesture of this world of vanity.

RE INFECTÂ

One thing I do regret and only one;
By token that I feel I'm drawing nigh
The ending of my day and soon must die,
My harvest yet unreaped, my work undone,
The riches of my soul revealed to none:
For poetry like plants is, that deny
To flower their best beneath a frowning sky,
Without their portion due of soil and sun.
So, like Kheyyám, with heart fulfilled I
Of vain regrets, for that the seed and germ
Of many a fair conceit in me I know,
Which, had Fate smiled and folk been less purblind.
With bloom and fruit had gladdened humankind,
But now must be the portion oi the worm.

NEARING PORT

Hope and sorrow, smiles and sadness,
Doubt and surety, glee and dole,
Hast thou fed thy full, my soul:
Grief galore and little gladness,
Goodness hast thou known and badness.
Pause and ponder now the whole,
In the distance since thy goal
Glimmers through Life's maze of madness.
Now thy day is near its ending,
Now thy travel home is tending,

Now Life's night is near its morrow,
Conscience clear and quiet mind,
Duty done, 'spite pain and sorrow,
Nothing else of worth thou'lt find.

MORS JANUA VITÆ

A lapse into the surgeless sea of Night;
Long devious wanderings in the darkling ways;
Some little blinded pause of blank amaze,
Of hands uplifted to the eternal height;
Some little straining of the astonied spright
For thought and cognizance, athwart the haze
Of nothingness, wherewith Death overlays
The deadened sense; and then a flood of light;
A conscience of the at last accomplished goal,
Of Past for ever past, of Present sole,
Without To-be abiding, in a clime
Of peace unchanging, quit of Space and Time,
Of all life's troubles ended for the soul,
Of Self resolved into the Eternal Whole.

MORTUIS DILECTIS

I.

You all, whom I have loved and who are dead,
Leaving me here to face the end alone,
As one, who, in mid-battle, all his own
Sees fall'n, and single, in the setting red,
Stands, with war-wearied, if unbated head,
These, that like flowers in me, unsought, unsown,
By field and garden, street and shore, have blown,
Or in the midnight hours upon my bed,
On your cold ashes, for you loved me well
And your hearts throbbed with mine in hopes and fears,
This wreath I lay of mingling smiles and tears,
A garland not alone of funeral flowers,
In many a variance plucked of sun and showers,
The tale of Love's rememorance to tell.

II.

Nay, they are yours: what time they grew in me,
Through many a glad and son)- day and night,
Your thought was with me, in the morning-white,
The evening-red; it was your harmony
I hearkened for, your eyes that did o'ersee
The growing line, your voice that bade me write;
And gathered now upon this page of white,
To you alone they dedicate shall be
And those true hearts, that music love and song,
For very song's alone and music's sake,
Nor to the poet reckon it for wrong,
On song-bird fashion music if he make.
As for the others, be they who they may,
They say. What say they? Marry, let them say!

John Payne – A Concise Bibliography

The Masque of Shadows & Other Poems (1870)
Intaglios; Sonnets (1871)
Songs of Life and Death (1872)
Lautrec: A Poem (1878)
The Poems of François Villon (1878)
New Poems (1880)
The Book of the Thousand Nights and One Night (1882–4) A translation in nine volumes
Tales from the Arabic (1884)
The Novels of Matteo Bandello, Bishop of Agen (1890) A translation in six volumes
The Decameron by Giovanni Boccaccio (1886) A translation in three volumes
Alaeddin and the Enchanted Lamp; Zein Ul Asnam and The King of the Jinn: (1889) editor and translator
The Persian Letters of Montesquieu (1897) Translator
The Quatrains of Omar Kheyyam of Nisahpour (1898)
Poems of Master François Villon of Paris (1900)
The Poems of Hafiz (1901) A translation in three volumes
Oriental Tales: The Book of the Thousand Nights and One Night (1901) A translation in fifteen volumes
The Descent of the Dove & Other Poems (1902)
Poetical Works (1902) Two volumes
Stories of Boccaccio (1903)
Vigil and Vision: New Sonnets (1903)
Hamid the Luckless & Other Tales in Verse (1904)
Songs of Consolation: New Poems (1904)
Sir Winfrith & Other Poems (1905)
Selections from the Poetry of John Payne (1906) selected by Tracy and Lucy Robinson
Flowers of France: Romantic Period (1906)
Flowers of France, The Renaissance Period (1907)
The Quatrains of Ibn et Tefrid (1908, second edition 1921)
Flowers of France: The Latter Days (1913)
Flowers of France: The Classic Period (1914)

The Way of the Winepress (1920)
Nature and Her Lover (1922)
The Autobiography of John Payne of Villon Society Fame, Poet and Scholar (1926)

www.ingramcontent.com/pod-product-compliance
Lightning Source LLC
Chambersburg PA
CBHW060138050426
42448CB00010B/2196